Wayward Tendrils of the Vine

Ian Maxwell Campbell

Introduced by Neal Martin

ACADEMIE DU VIN LIBRARY • CLASSIC EDITIONS

Contents

Académie du Vin Library Classic Editions

The Académie du Vin Library 'Classic Editions' lie at the very heart of the books we publish. When Steven Spurrier and I first talked about a new publishing imprint over lunch at our club (where else!), it was the older wine books we thought of first. These islands have been the heartland of wine appreciation, it seems, since Chaucer's time and there is much literature to draw from: wine writing that is elegant, informative, inspiring, often eccentric and frequently witty. Some of it feels dated now but that's part of its charm. What a shame it would be, we said to one another, if the words that inspired our own wine careers were lost to today's reader. Indeed, they shouldn't be! So while we at the Académie celebrate new authors, new adventures and new perspectives on our pages (and always will), we are now very proud to devote a new series of 'time capsule' titles to the wine writers who handed the job – if you can call it that – over to us.

I have shelves of these books, and quite a few favourites. Here, we welcome back Ian Maxwell Campbell, wine merchant and cricketer. What lives on is his special take on the wines he loved and his stories of the people he shared them with. It's incredible what you can still learn from him.

Hugh Johnson

About the Author

Ian Maxwell Campbell was born in 1870, a 'noble vintage year' as he liked to point out. His parents were both from Argyll, Scotland, but they moved south where Ian, along with seven of his brothers, was educated at Dulwich College. Ian's love of wine began at home as, being 'a fortunate fellow', both his parents were claret drinkers. He quickly found his palate, too, and learned to memorize flavours and impressions with accuracy. When sent to Bordeaux by his father's firm in 1882 (he was junior clerk at the venerable offices of Schröder and Schÿler) he discovered that others would listen to his opinions.

Via an army calling that saw him give service on the Western Front with the Argyll and Southern Highlanders (he'd reached the rank of lieutenant colonel by 1929) and a distinguished sporting career in which he played first class cricket alongside W G Grace and Malcolm Jardine (father of the more famous Douglas) Ian became a life-long connoisseur of wine, firmly seeing it as 'an object of art of such variety that, like the Universe itself, there is scarcely a beginning of the knowledge of it and certainly there is no end.'

In Ian's lifetime (1870–1954) he not only witnessed the damage of two world wars but also the havoc caused by the great phylloxera plague – he is one of the few writers to be able to chart the course of wine (not only Bordeaux) before and after these dramatic events. His political and cultural reference points along the way provide a fascinating backdrop to his memoirs – to name a few, Ian saw 'the great Sarah Berhardt' perform, crossed the Channel with William Gladstone and dined at lunch with T S Eliot (during which he was pressed to opine on the poems of Rudyard Kipling, and for a long while afterwards felt uncomfortable about it).

As a prominent member of the Wine Trade Ian was twice chairman of the Wine & Spirit Association and did his very best to spread the gospel of wine. And, as written in the cover of the 1948 edition of this book, 'a very good best that has been'.

'Some Press Opinions' from 1948

Wayward Tendrils of the Vine cannot fail to delight those who love wine and will prove a most valuable source of information to those who wish to learn about it.

'_Delightfully entertaining recollections of a lovable lover of wine... no book teaches one more about different wines, vintages and wine merchants, nor does any other book on wine make us better realize how rewarding a study and how fascinating a hobby wine is._' André Simon

'_The fascination of this book, apart from its wine lore, is the picture that is drawn all unawares of its writer, the most lovable of men, whose taste in wine betrays his character, a champion of high quality and the rare virtues of the saint and hero against mass-production and the nasty meannesses of the common man._' H Warner Allen

'_Now that good claret is so hard to come by, this lovable book will warm the heart and stimulate the mind almost as effectively._' James Laver

'_Colonel Ian Campbell, doyen of the London Wine Trade and probably the finest judge of wine in Britain, has celebrated his golden jubilee as a wine merchant by publishing his reminiscences. In this wise and entertaining book,_ Wayward Tendrils of the Vine, _one meets many famous men._' Peterborough in The Daily Telegraph

'_This is a gracious and pleasurable book, full of thanks for good Wine and good friends, both in and out of the Trade._' The Wine and Spirit Trade Record

Introduction
Neal Martin

Within wine literature, has there ever been a more evocative title than *Wayward Tendrils of the Vine?* I cannot think of one. The title of Ian Maxwell Campbell's book conjures images of a twisting and turning tendril growing day by day, oblivious to its destination except towards light. The title alone is a perfect allegory for how we learn about wine, how knowledge grows organically over time, never knowing what the next bottle will teach us, how it might alter preconceptions or where it might lead.

Published as the embers of World War II were still glowing, Campbell looks back at the end of what reads like an idyllic career in wine that spans the period of time from the mid-18th century up to his sober conjecture upon recent wartime vintages. Except for Professor Georges Saintsbury and Campbell's friend and mentor André Simon, there is no other source of first-hand encounters of wine that span the halcyon decades of the pre-phylloxera era. The reader must constantly remind themself that references to a '53 or '70 mean 1853 and 1870, not a century later.

The book serves as a precious porthole through which we can peer back into a bygone era whose rudimentary winemaking practices are not identical to contemporary approaches per se, but certainly chime with them. In that sense, Campbell's book is just as relevant now as it was back then. Look carefully and our author reveals secrets maybe lost in time, for example, the rumour circulating at the time that Haut-Brion might absorb the vines of La Mission Haut-Brion. Was that idle gossip or was that union seriously entertained in the aftermath of war?

Saintsbury's *Notes On A Cellar Book* set the template for wine literature upon publication in 1920. Alas, to put it kindly, it is not exactly a page-turner, as Campbell himself tactfully infers on the opening page where he apologizes for his own writing limitations, a self-described 'unskilled wielder of the pen'. On that, Campbell is wrong. He has a deft way with prose. Words flow naturally from his pen. We might never be able to compare the 1865 and 1870 Lafite Rothschild or the 1858 Cockburn, yet the manner of his writing, the affability that seeps through his mastery of the English language, makes the reader feel at ease, a welcome voyeur to bibulous tastings and dinners.

This book could read like a collector boasting about a mind-boggling array of legendary bottles, however there are no trumpets being blown here. Campbell is merely communicating the joy of wine to its then niche audience, with all its attendant rituals and conviviality. In this age when producers kowtow to consumers who demand immediate drinking fulfillment, his book is a pertinent reminder that nothing compares to a fine wine sculpted by time. It is almost impossible to read *Wayward Tendrils* and not feel the urge to start building a cellar to share with friends and family in the future.

Throughout the book, Campbell introduces us to the men – and it must be said that they are nearly all male, except for one woman admonished for lighting a cigarette as he poured an

1896 Vintage Port – with whom bottles are shared. Some are well-known like André Simon, the doyen of wine writers; Walter Berry of the merchant dynasty; cricketer W G Grace and prime-minister Sir Winston Churchill make their own cameos. Others pass through and we sketch in their personalities, imagine the cross-table banter and laughter that surely accompanied the wines. Nothing has changed in that respect, except thankfully in today's wine commentary the balance between is more equal.

The purview of the book is restricted to the Old World, predominantly Bordeaux and within that category, Left Bank over Right Bank. Poor old Petrus does not get a mention. This is not a factor of the author's myopia, rather the boundaries of what was classed as fine wine circa 1945. Even Burgundy, which Campbell confesses he has never been able to acquire intimacy with, appears in a minor role, as a quaint, bucolic region compared to aristocratic Bordeaux. Still, he clearly has experience of the great Burgundy wines of the early 19th century and I particularly enjoyed his serendipitous invention of 'Chablis Rosé': when a Dijon supplier shipped his wines in red burgundy casks, they arrived with a pinkish tinge. Instead of being rejected, they ended up a great success with consumers.

Campbell is clearly catholic in his tastes and presciently commends the few wines that he encountered from further afield such as Argentina, Chile and South Africa. I am sure he would be astonished at the number of countries that currently turn grapes into wine or the popularity of those countries' wines which in many ways have usurped Campbell's beloved Bordeaux.

Whilst today's vinous world is almost unrecognizable from the one that Campbell inhabited, many of its facets and principles remain true. And perhaps the one that underlies our enjoyment and passion for wine since time immemorial is summed up when our host advises: 'The quintessence of the enjoyment of good wine is the sharing of it with others.' That sums up *Wayward Tendrils of the Vine* perfectly. It resonates now more than ever. Just as Campbell wrote his book in September 1945 after six years of war, at a time when nobody knew how or when or if the world would recover, so in 2021, as we battle an invisible enemy in viral form, we look forward to a time when we can share bottles of wine again with friends and family.

April 2021

Wayward Tendrils of the Vine

The ways of the tendril are tortuous and indeterminate; it clings to any chance object that takes its fancy, but only to help it to reach a further and higher one: eventually it finds itself twisting and turning in the air with nothing more to cling to, alone, weary and neglected, having accomplished its task as guide and forerunner of the main stock from which it sprang and which it was born to serve.

CHAPTER 1

And so to Mark Lane

Home. General Cameron's Sherry. At 25 Mark Lane. 1887 Port. Off to Jerez and Soleras. Journeys and Congresses. Anti-Prohibition.

I have been pressed, even by people who call themselves my friends, to commit to writing some of the experiences of a well-spent (far-spent might sound better and more modest) life, particularly those connected with wine and the Wine Trade, of both of which I am a zealous admirer. These self-appointed counsellors hold up before me the example of the late Professor George Saintsbury, whose *Notes on a Cellar-Book*, by dealing with a subject of wellnigh universal interest, was probably more popular than almost any other of his literary productions. But then he was a practised writer and a man of encyclopaedic erudition, and his self-expression was both forceful and entertaining, although, between four walls, I have heard it whispered that his English was sometimes more basic than regal. Mine, I regret to say, is neither; but on the other hand, without any possible shadow of doubt, wine is a most fascinating topic about and around which to talk and write. Wine is an object of art of such variety that, like the Universe itself, there is scarcely a beginning of the knowledge of it and certainly there is no end. The discussion of wine, whether platonic, practical or epicurean, whether the outcome of mental or physical appetite, is always stimulating and worth while and sometimes may become sparkling and even illuminating; the freshness and novelty of it is ever undimmed and its charm and cosmopolitan friendliness is proverbial and for all ages. So let us talk about wine and the vine, and let the tendrils wander where they will: my memory is probably as wayward as their wanderings.

My father, who was a man of some importance, with a career of public usefulness and distinction, never wrote a book. When he was about fifty years of age and I about half that, I reminded him that our fellow countryman, Sir Walter Scott, only took up his magic pen at his own age and became a celebrated novelist and poet. My father did not take the implied compliment seriously and never wrote a book: I ask myself why then should I, who am only what my mother used to call 'a chip of the old block'. No invitation to do so has ever come from any of my own three sons; they are too well aware of their father's literary qualifications. They do not look for blackbird's eggs in a sparrow's nest! I begin to feel, even now, that, having strung together these few words, I am already on the slippery slope, but whether the further descent will be an easy one to the infernal regions remains to be seen. It may be just as well to explain how my connection with wine came about. I owe it, among many other good things, to my father. He started life as a Gunner, and possibly as a moderate amateur consumer of wine, and was at 'the Shop' somewhere about 1860–1861. He served with his battery in the Maori rising in New Zealand in 1864–66 under General Sir Duncan Cameron. He had many good stories to tell of the Campaign – among them one that once, when the Maoris were being shelled in their village or stockade, they came out under a white flag and asked for more ammunition as theirs had run out. They were, and are, great sportsmen, the Maoris, and it has been a privilege in later years to see them play Rugger. Mention of Sir Duncan Cameron gives me the chance of introducing a preliminary bit about wine, which will go to show how sentimental some of us can be.

Sir Duncan's great-niece gave for the Red Cross Sale of Wines, held in 1941 at Christie's wartime headquarters at Derby House (after their own place in King Street had been bombed), four half-bottles of sherry. These were the remnants of a gift from the King of Spain who had been a cadet at Sandhurst when Sir Duncan was Commandant. It was fitting that his niece should give them in aid of the Duke of Gloucester's Red Cross and St John Fund for victims of the Second World War. It seemed to me equally fitting that I, the only individual probably in the auction room who had seen the General, which I had done when I was a small lad at home, should bid for the four half-bottles. I did so and they fell to me for five pounds. Later on I tasted one. The wine, of undoubtedly magnificent quality, was of the darkest brown colour, sticky, pungent in bouquet of dead leaves and sweet with the flavour of burnt sugar. It was a delicious curiosity, though I confess that I would sooner drink, for every-day enjoyment, a glass of the more modest dry *fino* sherry. But sentiment was satisfied. I see that M. André Simon alludes to the last half-bottle in his recent most entertaining book *Vintagewise*.

And now to proceed. A year or two after my father had returned from New Zealand, which he always maintained offered some of the most beautiful scenery he knew, 'just like Scotland' as he would say, he married my mother. They were both from Argyll and were a wonderful couple, serving their generation together faithfully and happily (I never heard the suspicion even of a tiff between them) for nearly sixty years. In the course of twenty-one of these they added sixteen children to the population of the country, eight of whom were still alive in 1942. Gunner's pay would not go round! That must have become evident at an early stage of their married life, and my father took to business. Difficulties and hardships met him at every turn. He was not by nature cut out for a business career, but he persevered. Of his many troubles, including ourselves, we bright offspring knew nothing except that we were constantly changing house and that kind, red-faced, swollen-nosed old Mrs Lamont's periodical visits always happened to synchronize with the arrival of a new baby. Once only were we disappointed, almost affronted, at the non-appearance of a baby. We cross-questioned her but she fenced with words and left without any satisfactory explanation, which puzzled us greatly. The boy was stillborn. We were never told but later found it out from an entry in the family Bible. I must have been nearly thirty years of age, before, on a certain third of April, my mother said to me quietly, 'You know this is always a sad day for me: one of my dear little boys was born dead'. A loving and lovable mother; a true woman.

In 1882 we went to live in Upper Norwood so as to be near Dulwich College. Eight of us in succession went there. My brother Donald and I began in 1882 and the last one, Colin, left in 1906. It was, and is, a great school. I am sure the education there, equally from the national, social and academic point of view, was as certain as any obtainable elsewhere to produce intelligent and useful citizens, although there are, of course, exceptions. I remember when I was stationed at Ripon in the first 'Great War to end war' meeting a Colonel Burnside RAMG, an old Etonian, who, one day asked me what school I had been at. When I told him Dulwich, his reply was 'finest school in the country. When I was in India I always knew when I asked one of your old schoolfellows to do something, that the job would be well and thoroughly done.' I think he was right, but then I always do value the views of old Etonians. Cyril Wells, in the Dulwich cricket eleven with me, went there as a master, and his House was noted, I believe, as one of the most popular of its day.

After years of vicissitudes my father eventually found himself in the Wine Trade, of which he was to become a popular and respected member. Through the amalgamation of several firms he became a partner in Reid, Pye, Cunningham and Campbell at 25 Mark Lane, London, E C, Wine Merchants and Agents for Foreign Wine Shippers. That was in 1880 if my memory serves me well. All records were lost when the old offices and cellars were demolished by enemy action in the furious air raid of 10 May 1941, during which the House of Commons was also bombed; a never-to-be-forgotten date. In February 1889 my father introduced me to the firm, a long, clumsy, flabby-faced, rather shy and timid youth of eighteen years of age. At that time I hardly knew either the look or the taste of wine. I had only left Dulwich at the end of the previous summer term and had spent half the time since then at Beasley's establishment near Birmingham for the cure of stammering, a defect which has influenced the whole of my life and which, alas! still handicaps it at most inopportune moments. I must not morbidly dwell on this beyond saying that a stammerer always suffers from a lifelong sense of frustration, impotence and shame. *Ipse dixi*, and I ought to know. That, once on my feet, I have sometimes been able to string a few words coherently together has been a dispensation of Providence for which I am infinitely grateful.

My first job was the corking and labelling of the elegantly shaped sample bottles of Graham's 1887 Vintage Port: Queen Victoria's Jubilee year. It is a curious coincidence when I write this that the 3s 6d per glass vintage port, now 'on tap' at the hotel where my wife and I are staying over fifty years later, is the identical wine to which the above sentence refers. I became so saturated with the smell and taste of that 1887 that it has ever since been my yardstick in assessing the quality of young vintage port. It was not a truly great vintage but its wines were pleasant and attractive. Some poetry is rather like that – also some human beings.

I was soon however shipped off to Spain to study the sherry business in Jerez de la Frontera. My elder brother, Don, and I left Tilbury Docks in the same steamer, P & O ss *Nepaul*, he for Amoy, I for Gibraltar. Our good parents, the turtle doves, came to see us off, very sad and watery-eyed at losing two such radiant members of their big progeny. I spent rather over a year in Jerez, employed in the *bodega* of Richard C Ivison, an exceptionally fine judge of sherry. If I then acquired what I think is called a discriminating palate, I owe much to his teaching and example. In these reminiscences of mine I shall try to keep away from technical detail as much as possible, both for the sake of my lay readers and to avoid the exposure of a deplorable and indefensible ignorance, but I must mention that it came as a surprise almost unbelievable to me, that one sherry vineyard could produce so many different styles of sherry in the outcrop of one vintage. This was no doubt what gave rise to the 'solera' system, about which so much has been written by the experts and so little understood by the public. This failure of effort does not very much matter so long as it is realized that 'solera' symbolizes a system for maturing sherry and is not itself the description of one type of wine.

What a volume of pleasant things I could write about Jerez and the Jerezanos, both Spanish and British! and it is not unlikely that some of my generous friends and varied experiences out there may receive a fuller tribute later on in these or other pages. Mine was a very happy time there and I met with wonderful and not-to-this-day-forgotten kindness. Fat and olive-tinted, after acquiring the good habit of drinking sherry through all meals, I returned home via Bordeaux, where I met my father and mother. Thanks to the place they held in the estimation of our Principals there, Messrs Schröder and Schÿler & Cie, I had a most friendly welcome and eventually received the unexpected offer of a temporary seat in their offices (they always say *bureaux* with an x in France) as soon as I was able to accept it. One of the partners of the firm kissed me on both cheeks when the offer was made. He was Camille Kirstein, an indefatigable worker and very clever taster of claret, but he was far from beautiful: in fact I doubt much if any friend I ever had was more unattractive, I could almost say repellent, to look at. But he had a kindly heart. He stood well over six feet with the limbs of some huge denizen of the forest. I think he owed the pachydermatous appearance of his skin to a complaint called elephantiasis, but I am no dermatologist; and I do not like being kissed by men or elephants, but Frenchmen do come at you so unexpectedly. *C'est l'élan français* that has so often carried them to victory! Madame Kirstein, on the other hand, was a pretty, elegant and charming lady, but, like so many other friends of my young days, she and her husband have both passed on.

Nearly two years went by before I was able to accept Messrs Schröder and Schÿler & Company's invitation. I spent about a year and a half in Bordeaux with them and would have considered myself a fool indeed, and worse than a fool, had I not profited by the opportunity to imbibe both the wines and the knowledge that came my way. My stay in that cosmopolitan city was a period of concentrated education and experience of inestimable value to me in my career with the wine trade and in numerous other directions. Visits to Reims, Dijon and Oporto, all enshrouded now with the glamour of delightful memories, helped to fill my storehouse of vinous information. I have to thank my connection with the wine trade for practically all my travelling abroad. On many occasions my wife has accompanied me and always on those on which, as one of Great Britain's representatives, I attended the annual conference of *La Ligue Internationale des Adversaires de la Prohibition*, now in a state of suspended animation since Finland and the United States of America discovered in the hard school of experience that men – and women – will defy the law if the law denies them the reasonable use of God's gifts to mankind or otherwise encroaches upon their rightful liberties. Man shall not live by bread alone, neither shall Man live by water alone if he wishes to drink something he considers to be better for him.

We attended congresses in Paris, Budapest and Copenhagen and also had one in London during the time I was a member of the Executive Committee of the League. During the London Congress, which took place in 1933, there was a remarkable exhibition, which I was lucky enough to get Francis Berry and André Simon to organize, of drinking vessels, housed in the Vintners' Hall; this was opened by the Princess Alice, Countess of Athlone, who, in the course of a charming address, said: 'It gives me great pleasure, as the daughter of a vintner, and the wife of a vintner, to open this unique exhibition. A particular interest which attaches to it is that the exhibits are largely of English creation and English make, ranging from the work of the craftsmen whose work graced the festive board 4,000 years ago, down to the beautiful piece which was completed only two days ago. To some minds, the drinking of wine is associated only with the consumption of alcohol to excess, but, as Shakespeare said, "Wine is a good familiar creature if it be well used". The artists who designed the beautiful goblets and glasses did not work for them, but strove to suit the vessel to the colour and quality of the choice wines which were to be put before men of taste, who were able to enjoy the wine the more for the beauty of the vessel in which it was served.'[1]

At Copenhagen, Professor Brandt of Sweden, later, I believe, connected with K L G plugs, who attended one of our sessions, made some very unwise and provocative remarks which roused his audience to hostile demonstrations. Ernest Oldmeadow passed me a note calling my attention to the disgraceful utterance, and our President, Baron Raymond de

---

[1] Extract from 'History of Wine Drinking' which appeared in *Harper's Wine and Spirit Gazette*, 24 June 1933.

Luze, heatedly denounced Dr. Brandt and refused to accept his paper. As one of Raymond's loyal vice-presidents I jumped to the rostrum and stoutly seconded the denunciation amid excited applause, and the incident, short, swift and cyclonic, was closed. Sir Alec Walker, that shrewd, reticent Scot, did not criticize my own action but came up afterwards to me and said 'these excitable little Frenchmen: just like them', and the cap fitted. One of the Copenhagen papers next morning came out with a cartoon depicting Raymond and myself throwing bottles at the distinguished professor! It was in Copenhagen that, at a semi-official dinner, I sat next to the elderly and eminent Czech professor, Dr. Stoclasa, who travelled with two lady secretaries and a whole collection of ribbons, *écharpes* and decorations, which he wore on every possible occasion. He had honoured the rostrum during one of the *séances* that day and had given an oration in German which no one, apparently, not even the German delegates present, had been able to understand. All I was able to pick up was the word 'alcool' at the end of each sentence. He was so dignified and awe-inspiring, however, that my timid spirit sank a little when I found myself sitting next to him at the dinner-table in the evening. I inquired optimistically whether he spoke English, but he brushed the soft impeachment aside by saying, not so well as German or French, and I think he named several other languages. So we spoke bad French together, and my inferiority complex disappeared entirely when I saw him pouring the fine claret into his equally fine champagne. *'Pourquoi faites-vous ça?'* I queried. *'Parce que je trouve que ça donne de l'énergie'*, he replied with an eye of *savoir faire*, and when I came to think of it I remembered that I had heard a senior officer say that young fellows in the army used to enjoy mixing champagne and claret together many years ago. I have never done it myself but I have tasted sparkling burgundy and that has been a sufficient deterrent. Actually I suppose that drinking claret after champagne, which is not an uncommon practice of mine, should have the same physiological effect as the old professor's unorthodox but, according to him, energizing mixture.

Whether our conferences and discussions played any great part in persuading both Finland and the United States to relinquish the temporary experiment of prohibition, I know not, nor does it much matter. The common sense of civilized, God-fearing people, whether they be Finnish or American, or any other nationality, will always outlive the short-sighted fanaticism of perhaps well-meaning but much mistaken busybodies and emotional reformers, whose limited perception of relative values is only equalled by a pigheaded and mischievous obstinacy. God created the wine-producing vine and distributed it over the face of the globe for the use and enjoyment of Man. The Founder of Christianity patronized wine and sanctified wine. The Bible makes constant reference to wines and strong drinks, acknowledging, in so many words as well as by implication, the benefit of their use and the evil consequences of their abuse. Wine is only one of many gifts mandated to humanity by an all-wise Providence for our enjoyment but not our misapplication, to inculcate in us the great lessons of self-control and self-respect without which Man would be beastlike and good for nothing.

CHAPTER 2

The Tendrils Travel

Definition of Wine. The Way of the Navy. Bordeaux Bureaux. Value of Memory. Judging Wine. A Deplorable Individual. Royan and a Heat Wave. '21 Cheval Blanc. 'Balance' in Wine. 'Ordinaire.' Derby Days. Pre-Phylloxera Vintages. 1888 Misses a Chance, and gets one.

Claret for many hundreds of years has meant, in Great Britain, the red wine of Bordeaux, but the name is now being appropriated by other wine-producing countries. Without any intention to be controversial, when I use the word 'claret' I mean the red wine of Bordeaux. One can say and write more about claret than about any other wine.

Claret is a perfectly natural, completely fermented red wine. Claret of all wines gives the truest expression of grape juice. That does not imply any reflection on other wines. Far from it: they all have their place in the sun. Definitions are difficult: I know it from experience. In the days when Government smiles and favours encouraged the manufacture in this country of 'wines' made from dried or dehydrated grapes, to which could be added water – and other ingredients – one or two members of the Wine and Spirit Association were asked to formulate a definition of WINE. After consulting the various and not dissimilar definitions officially recognized in different wine-producing countries of Europe, we came out with the following:

'Wine is the alcoholic beverage obtained from the fermentation of the juice of freshly gathered grapes the fermentation of which has been carried through in the district of its origin and according to local tradition and practice.'

This was adopted by the Association but has never received the official imprimatur although strangely enough it has been left for a Socialist Minister of Food to take the first intelligent interest in it. Directly I showed it to Sir Ben Smith he asked for a copy to help him to rid the country of all the spurious, semi-alcoholic vegetable concoctions which, assuming vinous nomenclature, deceived the PEOPLE (Sir Ben is a true democrat) during the recent war years. The definition may not be perfect; it has been described as too academic and too long. As a matter of fact, had we said that 'Wine is the alcoholic beverage obtained from the fermentation of the juice of freshly gathered grapes', the definition would have been more concise and perhaps equally effective. We in the wine trade have not been able to prevent the increased manufacture of 'British Sweets' which are still allowed to be sold as wines. On the contrary, during the War 'British Wines' have been sometimes made from apples, and goodness knows what other components, and foisted on a thirsty public as Port Type or Sherry Type – and so on – *ad nauseam*: yes, literally, AD NAUSEAM!

A taste for claret is an acquired one. French children inherit it because, from early childhood, claret, with water added, is their daily beverage. Those of us who are not French generally have to go through an experimental period of fluctuating opinion. There is no need for me to say that this trial of the palate, and the more sensitive the palate the keener the trial, is applicable to many other good things besides claret. Oysters, caviare, marmalade, sweetbreads, beer, cheese and boiled eggs (but I think I was unlucky with these last when young) were among the articles of diet I once abhorred and had to learn to like. I succeeded! Most of those who give good claret a fair trial also succeed. I myself was the most fortunate of fellows. My father and mother were both claret drinkers and, incidentally, they both lived to a good old age. On my mother's fiftieth birthday my father opened for her his last bottle of the famous 1864 Château Lafite, most perfect of clarets. All those of us at home were seated round the big table enjoying the happy party when one of my younger brothers, then Midshipman Campbell, now Admiral Campbell, burst breezily into the room. 'Darling boy,' said my mother, 'fancy coming on my birthday' – she had seventeen hearts, my mother, and husband and children were all included – 'sit here, next to me; look what your father has opened for me, his last bottle of 1864 Lafite' and, lack-a-day, she pushed her glass towards him. The gallant young sailor took the glass and promptly poured the contents down his throat as if it had been a cup of tea. Then, with innocent satisfaction, he ejaculated: 'That's the way we have in the Navy, father.' I watched my father's face grow scarlet as a Turner sunset, but, with characteristic self-control, he said nothing. It must have been a sad shock to him. Jim has learned better!

I went to Bordeaux in privileged circumstances early in 1892, soon after I came of age. As already mentioned, I entered the offices of Schröder and Schÿler & Cie, *maison fondée en 1739*, the oldest established firm of claret shippers in Bordeaux. My father and his partners were their agents in England, and, although I went to them as a junior clerk, I was almost treated like a junior partner, and can never be grateful enough to Oscar and Albert Schÿler and Camille Kirstein (the one who kissed me!) for the consideration, kindness and instruction I received from them all.

After a very short time I began to find my feet and also, I hope it is not conceited to say so, my palate. I found gradually that my opinion on claret was listened to and, even then, acted upon – at times. Albert Schÿler was my chief mentor and an intimate personal friend of my father's. He was a popular, well-nourished, gay and genial man under middle age at that time, who knew the English language and the British Isles intimately and loved them. He had a well-balanced, tolerant, rather cynical outlook on life, but was one of the most generous and kindhearted men you could meet. He gave me every chance and taught me much. Soon after I had settled down in the office he showed me some old clarets and made me taste them and then told me what they were. I cannot remember them all now, but one was the 1878 Château Palmer-Margaux and I liked it. It must have been a few weeks later that I was dining with Madame Vve Schÿler, the mother of Oscar and Albert, who had all her family of sons and daughters with their spouses and elder children round her every Thursday evening – a real jolly family gathering. We drank our '*pour le soif*' light claret and one or two others, at the identity of which members of the family all made shots. I held my tongue but thought the more. One claret in the course of one of these dinners I thought I recognized and, having seen some of the family using their shirt-cuffs – boiled shirts being *de rigueur* in those days – as memorandum blocks, I put down on my shirt-cuff '1878' but said nothing until, after the company had expressed their different opinions, Albert announced that it was the 1878 Château Palmer-Margaux. Then, with all the abandon and jubilant pride of a winner, I shot out my shirt-cuff and said, 'There! 1878' – and showed it across an intervening diner to Albert. He was clearly very delighted, and the others began to take *le jeune anglais* (not *le jeune écossais* to them!) more seriously. I may say *en passant* that Madame Vve Schÿler had invited me with most charming grace to join the gathering every Thursday and make myself one of the family. What luck! What a privilege!

I mention this little incident to illustrate the fact that one of the qualifications for becoming even a passable judge of claret, or indeed of any wine, is a good memory and being able to memorize for a length of time taste, flavour and impression accurately and exactly. Anybody may like or dislike a particular claret and have as much right to his opinion as the greatest expert, but to be a reliable judge he must know the whys and wherefores; he must be able to distinguish, and point out to others, shades of difference and degrees of perfection, or rather imperfection, for perfection in this world, even in wine, is rare indeed. A wine may have great qualities and yet be far from perfect: you should know why. Wine is a living entity and, because of that, two bottles of a wine may have been drawn and bottled from the same cask at the same time and stored in the same bin till they are both taken out on the same evening, equally carefully decanted and served side by side, and there yet will almost certainly be a perceptible difference between them. Wherein and why? Do not twins differ? All growth in life begets difference and divergence. Some people will like the one and some prefer the other: and the majority when asked for a reason will simply say, 'I don't know but I like that one best' (it's *their* grammar, not mine!). The wise judge of all arts, the expert, the critic, will generally look in the first place for faults and be able confidently to point them out, but he will also see merit if it is there and be able to point that out too. So should it be with the really good judge of a wine, and if, for educational purposes, it is necessary to encroach on the bin of some vinous treasure, he will not hesitate and, as reward of his sacrifice, will for days, months, perhaps for years, have an appreciative recollection of the treasure's colour, bouquet and flavour, and of some friend's companionship – a pleasant memory.

Apropos of perfection and imperfection, anybody may drink and enjoy a wine that is not perfect; most of us 'wine-bibbers' do it every day: the deplorable individual is he who will, like Mr Mountchesney, drink a wine that is definitely bad and enjoy it. I remember such a one (do I not?) soon after my wife and I were married. We were just sitting down to dinner one Sunday evening in Roseneath, our little suburban villa in Upper Norwood, which, by the way, witnessed the birth of our three boys, when the front door bell rang and in walked an old friend of my father's to pay us a call. Of course he was invited to share our potluck and accepted. I scampered downstairs in haste to our modest cellar, picked out a bottle of what I considered the best claret I then had – the 1892 Château Palmer-Margaux – and hastily decanted it into the 'Duck', a not unusual shape for a claret decanter in those days, and handed it over to our parlourmaid. In due course she filled my wife's glass and then that of our guest who, before you could say 'Jack Robinson', had literally gulped its contents down. 'Well Ian', said he, 'that is beautiful, delicious. I knew I would get a good glass of wine in your house.' By this time our little Hebe

17

had poured some into my glass which I lifted to my nose before drinking. It was like coming up against the wall of a cork factory and my nose, always rather pernickety, recoiled as if struck by a prizefighter. Fortunately, my wife, who is as quick as anybody I know at detecting any suspicion of 'cork', had said nothing and I was able to hand our enthusiastic guest the decanter and tell him to drink the lot as I could get more of the wine any day I wanted it. He took me at my word, cleared the decanter and enjoyed every drop of its contents. Now, he was a very rich man but ruined all the big dinner parties he and his wife gave by erroneously and ignorantly serving the cheapest and nastiest of drink, as I was to discover later from personal experience. But I learned two lessons on that occasion, over forty years ago, which I have never forgotten. First, at the expense even of time, you must see that your wine is clean and good before you serve it, and secondly, do not open your best wine unless you know that your guest will appreciate it. I called in question whether I had exhibited true Christian virtue in allowing a guest, a man at least double my own age, to drink bad wine, but if there was any display of bad taste it was on his part and, moreover, he was so enthusiastic that I hadn't the heart to pour cold water on the much eulogized wine.

It may seem curious that I should have considered a wine of 1892 – an unrecognized vintage – to be one of the best in my little cellar, but I always liked Palmer, and my friends Schröder and Schÿler had purchased the 1892 monopoly of the 'Growth', as vineyards are designated and classified in Bordeaux. Moreover I was in Bordeaux during practically the whole of 1892 and this wine itself developed surprisingly well. All things considered, however, 1892 vintage was a failure. The heat wave that culminated on August 8 in a phenomenal shade temperature of, I was told, 108° Fahr., scorched the vines and destroyed any hope there might have been of satisfactory fermentation. My friends bought the monopoly of the Château de Parempuyre of that year as well, with the kindly desire of giving his first order to a young *courtier*, or broker, called Damade, who had just come into the Bordeaux business. Their laudable intention however led to the law courts as the wine indulged in a secondary fermentation and went to pieces and, I have no doubt, to vinegar in double-quick time. Damade, whom I had the pleasure of seeing again only a few years ago, became one of the leading brokers in the Bordeaux market and he still talks French with what I should call the Oxford accent. I was spending my holidays with the Schÿler family that August of 1892 at Pontaillac just beyond Royan-les-Bains at the mouth of the river Gironde; beautiful sands by a beautiful sea. I was Madame Vve Schÿler's guest, and the party; spread over various villas and chalets, consisted of innumerable relations, cousins and kinsfolk of all ages – something like a clan gathering in the Highlands of Scotland. We spent most of that memorable day disporting ourselves in the sea, rowing out some distance and upsetting the boat, and all that sort of thing, little imagining that the glorious sunshine which so glowingly dominated our enjoyment was searing and scorching the luscious fruit upon which the prosperity of our hosts and neighbours so largely depended. 'Sometime too hot the eye of heaven shines', and this was one of those occasions.

The vintage of 1921 was a sort of counterpart of 1892 as, owing to fierce summer sunshine, the vines were *brulés* or burnt, though I have no record of any particular day of the year. The vintage was pronounced a failure with one brilliant exception, well known to claret lovers, the Château Cheval Blanc. This remarkable wine had a flowery smell, or 'bouquet', as it is called, and was very full-flavoured, with a touch of burnt grapes in the flavour, and much sweeter than the majority of clarets had been for many years. Its deep rich colour and exceptional all-round merits were at once recognized and the price of it rose steeply even while it was quite young. I have always feared that such excess of sweetness would unbalance the wine and turn it to vinegar, and one or two bottles I have drunk or, rather, joined in drinking have indicated a somewhat acetic tendency. But I have had the wine again quite lately (in 1943) and most thoroughly enjoyed it. My advice, for what it is worth, to those who have the wine, is to drink it while the going is so good. Of course the success of the Cheval Blanc not unnaturally led later on to other proprietors of well-known châteaux placing their erstwhile discarded 1921 products on the market, but I eye these, so to speak, deathbed repentances, with suspicion as I would most such tergiversations under similar circumstances. All the same, I have recently enjoyed the '21 Latour, not burnt, at Berry Bros & Rudd's hospitable luncheon table, and also the Domaine de Chevalier, a red Graves wine that is frequently very good in what we call 'off' vintages.

I have just remarked in reference to the 1921 Ch (short for château and more often used) Cheval Blanc that I feared the 'excess of sugar would unbalance the wine' and lead to its disintegration and downfall. In all wines a *perfect* 'balance' may mean the approach to that unattainable will-o'-the-wisp perfection, but a *good* 'balance' is absolutely essential: and by 'balance' is meant, untechnically speaking, the relatively correct proportion in the wine of all vinous ingredients, mineral, vegetable, and chemical, such as water, sugar, tannin, alcohol, ethers, and so on, requisite to show health, strength, quality and promise of tip-top normal development. Unless a wine has that good balance it may charm for a while but it will not endure: and the better the breed of the wine, the more necessary the good balance. From long and oft-times bitter experience the vineyard proprietors generally know more or less the *datum* lines between the good, the doubtful and the bad balance, though it must never be forgotten that wine is a living entity; that it has been known to recover completely from infantile delicacy and what might be called teething ailments, and that on the other hand robustness and early promise have often proved fallacious. Risks must be run in viticulture as in other enterprises. One of the pleasures of life is the purchase and laying down of a wine with some uncertainty about its future: your opinion against your friend's perhaps, and both of you, even more rashly, against that of your wine merchant. You cannot accumulate a good cellar stock unless you speculate.

Of course the need for the perfect balance is not so necessary in the selection of everyday claret, the wine we used to buy at about 1s 6d a bottle and now, thanks to rapacious Chancellors of the Exchequer, at many shillings more, even in peacetime. You look for a wine that pleases you at the moment and of which you can buy a further quantity or a 'follow' when you want it. I am a believer in every healthy man and woman who may be classified as a brainworker enjoying his or her daily quota, be it pint or quart, of claret, as a pleasant, beneficial, inexpensive (in more normal times) and agreeably stimulating beverage, even if the taste for and appreciation of it may have to be acquired: in this country, as I have remarked before, it rarely comes naturally. I know no better thirst-quencher than a big glass of claret, without the accompaniment of food. The wine I recommend for daily drinking is not one of the great classic *châteaux*, but rather an ordinary, cheap, young, but equally genuine '*petit bourgeois*' or lower-graded wine, of which hundreds are vintaged in the Gironde every year. P G H Fender, the cricketer, discussing a *bourgeois* we were drinking, said it was 'so sweet it might almost be a *bourgeoise!*' Talking of ordinary, or more properly *ordinaire*, as the Bordelais habitually term such wines, calls to my mind a story told by my father of dining at a certain London restaurant. As usual he called for a wine-list and turned at once to the 'Clarets': he was highly amused to see the list of clarets headed by

Bordeaux, ordinaire, 2s 6d a bottle
Bordeaux, très ordinaire, 3s 6d a bottle,

a demonstration of the danger of a little knowledge. I am sure I have perpetrated linguistic errors of a similar nature, but it is only human to remember rather the occasions on which others have done so. My lately retired partner Nevile Reid and I together visited Dijon to see our Burgundy Principals. We dined one evening at the house of their then senior partner, M. Moser, who, although a Swiss himself, gave us a dinner worthy of France and the great gastronomic reputation of the City of the old Burgundian Dukes. Among several other wines served, both red and white, was a Chablis Moutonne, I think of 1889 or approximate vintage, and towards the end of dinner there was some of this wine left and some also of a red wine, but I cannot remember what. Moser asked us both which we would have and, as is my wont, I chose the red, but Nevile said, with the deliberation of one who knows what's what, '*Je prendrai un petit gout de mouton!*' Our good host's features never relaxed. I fear to ask how often my host has had to exercise similar control over his countenance on my account: *maintes fois je parie!*

Moser was a good fellow and a straight one, risen from clerk to senior partner: he was also a fine judge of the wines of the Côte d'Or. My wife and I took him with us as one of a party to the Derby one year. He entered thoroughly into the spirit of this most popular of all public gatherings, and, when the gipsy lady asked leave to tell his fortune by the palm of his hand, he acquiesced with glee. Taking his hand and holding it she looked at him archly for a few seconds and then exclaimed: 'Oh, naughty colonel!' He was in ecstasies, and many a letter did he write me thereafter signed, 'The naughty Colonel'. Stories of Derby Day are manifold and in them history repeats itself like an echo amid the mountains, but the unusual and not unamusing episode of Edwin King must be told. Edwin was managing director of Messrs Stephen Smith & Co the proprietors of 'Keystone' Australian wines, and shortly after the end of the First World War he was elected President of the Wine Trade Club, a popular, generous president, prone to make the most comical remarks with an air of completely unaffected innocence. The Club had a Derby Day Dinner when several of us who had not been to Epsom would join the party that had. On the occasion to which I allude we had all assembled except Edwin King who had gone off with the festive party to the races but got lost and was left behind. As he was chairman, we waited dinner for him and at last he turned up looking crestfallen and sorry for himself in his inimitably waggish way. Of course he had to make a speech: he related how on arriving at Epsom he had volunteered to buy the ice-cream for the party and had gone off with the tin bucket to do so. He got his tin pail filled with beautiful pink strawberry ice-cream and started for the pre-arranged *rendez-vous* to rejoin the party, but no trace of them was to be found. He spent the rest of the hot sunny day trudging about with the pailful, jostled by the myriad merrymakers, missing all the races, not to mention his luncheon, escaping by inches being run over by waggonettes and charabancs, in a vain search for his companions. They apparently had also been looking for him, as for a needle in a haystack, and had finally given him up, but the story of unrequited self-sacrifice, told in Edwin's most whimsical manner, was a masterpiece, and our hilarious appreciation and applause must have cheered him a lot and made up for his day's disappointment. Poor Edwin! Too early in life he passed away, after a long and tedious illness, much regretted by all who knew him best and his simple kindly heart. But I digress. It is the fault of the *très ordinaire*.

I was one of the luckiest of fellows to have been in Bordeaux in the early 'nineties before they, too, became 'naughty'. In 1892 the famous vintage of 1875 was at its best, and what a best! The fine, almost equally famous, 1874 was running strongly but most of its backers had begun to realize that it lacked something of the superlatively unsophisticated charm and sunniness of the '75.

The wines of 1878, although sweet and well-constituted, were at that time considered to be coarse and common and not in the same class as '74 and '75, while 1877s, light and elegant with just the *soupçon* of a squeeze of lemon in the final farewell, were expected to be the natural, if less captivating, successors to 1875, but fell far short. And yet, in all justice, and because 1877 is André Simon's birthyear, I must record that, in June 1945, Hugh Rudd, Kenneth Upjohn and I, at 3 St James's Street, after a bottle of 1917 Ch Lafite, enjoyed, to our surprise and delight, a bottle of 1877 Ch Lafite which I noted at the time as 'no lemon, very good, still fresh, sweet and young'.

Those wines of 1871 that still adorned the cellars of the few were there to delight the most sensitive nose and most exacting palate. When they were first made France was in a state of disturbance and the vintage was quite neglected, a veritable Cinderella; and, like that popular heroine, it proved to be a gem of purest ray serene that did not for ever blush unseen – and such a blush – for it received princely honour amongst connoisseurs of wine, a great many of whom declared it to be the most completely perfect and winsome claret they had ever known. I doubt if many of the proprietors, even of the classed growths, bottled their wines of 1871 at the châteaux, so little did they, or indeed anyone else at the time, appreciate the unique quality hidden beneath a rather too modest and diaphanous outward appearance. They followed too soon after the fine aristocratic 1869s and the pachydermatous 1870s, of which more anon. My own firm in London bought (before my time!), if not the whole crop, a good part of the 1871 Ch Latour, bottled it in London and started selling it to wine merchants at 26s a dozen! It was a superb wine with a perfume of summer flowers and a delicate flavour not unlike that of ripe nectarines. When my people put the price up to 36s a dozen they almost felt like pioneers of a Black Market! But the wine's development and repute proved that they were fully justified and might have been a bit more greedy.

All these may be called pre-phylloxera vintages though it is possible that that nasty pernicious little American bug had already, in 1878, begun to afflict the vines. I doubt very much whether the vineyards have yet entirely recovered from the phylloxeric infection. The beetle, or bug, attacks the roots of the vines, and in the Gironde practically every one of these had to be dug up and destroyed while cuttings of the doomed plants were grafted on to clean immune young American stock: *c'était l'amende honorable.*

The vines have done their best and with age will, it is sincerely to be hoped, regain a large part of their pristine virtue.

The 1888s made a brave effort to return to type and very nearly succeeded, but alas! the reconditioned vines lacked strength to resist the second-front attacks of another aggressive and destructive enemy, mildew. As young wines the 1888s were very attractive, deliciously scented and with a pronounced flavour of hothouse grapes, but this flavour was the camouflage used by the mildew to deceive the overtrusting. The wines faded more or less rapidly away (though a very occasional bottle of the Ch Margaux and one or two others may still be drinkable) and a great many keen and intelligent merchants and shippers of Bordeaux burnt their fingers badly. One firm which had plunged and lost heavily on the expensive, stout-bodied, tannin-bound wines of 1870, which took over fifty years to reach maturity and become drinkable, now went to the opposite extreme and plunged heavily on the light, ephemeral, mildewed wines of 1888, most of which died in childhood. It goes to show that even the experts may err when dealing with the uncertainty of life to which the whole realm of creation is subject. But assuredly the 1888s were most deceptive when young and seemed as if they might well be the destined successors of 1875, a title which 1877 had failed to achieve. One day I was brought into the tasting room at Schÿler's office where I found three of the partners discussing half a dozen samples of claret. This was of course in 1892. Camille Kirstein said to me: 'We want you to look at these wines without knowing what they are; a Paris restaurant has finished all its stock of 1875 claret and wants to follow with the best we can do. We want you to represent the *restaurateur* and tell us which of these wines, of different vintages is most like and will best follow a '75.' I tasted them (my palate was more reliable then than now) and picked out one. It turned out to be an 1888, the Pichon-Longueville, one of the youngest wines, if I remember rightly, on the board, but certainly the only one at all resembling, in bouquet, flavour and sweetness, a '75, in my opinion, and apparently I was with the majority. Whether the *restaurateur* whom I represented put it on his list as '1875' history does not relate!

CHAPTER 3

Histoires Bordelaises

Stories of Mildew. Of '77 and '78. Saintsbury Club Stories, and Others.
André Simon. A Cockburn Dinner. Heavy Clarets and Light. Stories of
'70 Margaux. Of '64 Lafite. Sizes of Bottles. Barry Neame's Little Game.

I have passed over 1872, 1873 and 1876 of that wonderful
decade, all moderately good but outclassed. 1879, 1880 (with
the exception of the Mouton Rothschild), 1881 (inky and dry),
1882, 1883, 1884, 1885 and 1886 were all thin, mawkish and
more or less badly diseased, and it may have been due to this
long, wearisome and expensive succession of failures, the result
no doubt of constitutional weakness in the vine, that the taste
for claret began to totter, and some proprietors, and at least one
firm of shippers, well known in those days, took to pasteurizing
their clarets to retain the sugar and check both growth and
decay. It was a criminal interference, in my opinion, with the
whole time-honoured production of a wine that has made its
reputation and will only retain its reputation on the impeccability of its natural and complete fermentation. Impatience with
the vagaries of Nature is not thus to be expressed. Some people
prophesied a great future for vintage 1884, and one Frenchman
in London, called Michaud, I think, bet a silk hat that it would
develop more finely than 1875! He lost his silk hat and his

reputation as a prophet, as the vintage was as full of mildew as any and collapsed hopelessly. It is true that Eddie Harvey gave us a bottle of an '84 one day in Bristol, but more as a curiosity than a treat. It was in about 1930 and the wine had not yet fallen so low as so many of its contemporaries. Mildew gives the wine a pinkish tinge and to the novice tastes sweet and not unpleasant, but eventually it palls and its admirer finds the apparent sweetness to be sickly (sicklied o'er with the pale cast of pinkeye) and the final taste of the wine mousey, acrid and disagreeable. With experience one can generally spot even the very slightest tendency towards mildew. In opposition to many devotees of claret, including my good friend the late Maurice Healy, to whose Irish brogue and humour it was so delightful to listen anywhere, even on the air, I always maintained that the 1912 vintage was marred by mildew. To a dinner of the 'Odde Volumes' at which General Sir Ian Hamilton and I were among his own four or five personal guests, Maurice had brought two magnums of the 1912 Ch Latour, to convince me that the wine was not mildewed. Both he and I were very much disappointed when Sir Ian, good Gordon Highlander and ideal dispatch-writer, said he did not dare to drink claret and asked for whisky, but the rest of us accounted for the magnums of the Latour, which in my opinion were distinctly tainted, if not as badly as some other wines of the vintage; and even Maurice, though more obstinate than most people I have met, eventually agreed that a 'peculiar flavour' about it might be mildew. Ch Latour and its neighbours at Pauillac, Ch Lafite and Ch Mouton Rothschild, often survive the ravages of sickness or disease that do ill to the lighter and tenderer wines of St. Julien, Margaux and Cantenac. Maurice was not a wine-drinker when the 'egregious eighties' were on the wine-lists or he would have known for certain.

One curiously attractive claret of 1912 was the Clos Fourtet, the well-known vineyard in the heart of the famous little town of St Emilion. We had a fair amount of it in our cellars in Mark Lane and used to have it up at some of our luncheon parties at 'No. 25', now levelled to the ground 'by enemy action' except for an inner wall showing two of our fireplaces, one on the first and one on the second floor. 'Annie' Irish, so called since his Oxford days and now head of the old firm of Christopher & Co, one of the most-honoured men in the wine trade, was lunching with us there one day and had a bottle of the '12 Fourtet. He smacked his lips. 'I like that,' said he; 'what's your price? I'll take some.' 'But it's mildewed,' I expostulated, for once in a way letting friendly frankness get the better of commercial instinct! 'If so,' he replied, 'I like mildew,' and he took so many dozens. Not many weeks had elapsed before he telephoned to us, and my partner Nevile Reid, who had been at Brasenose with him, answered. 'I don't want to speak to you,' came Irish's voice, 'I want particularly to speak to Ian.' I was put through and the greeting I got was: 'Have you any more of that Château Mildew left? My friends seem to like it.' I would not for a moment say Irish was mistaken: he is a very discerning judge of claret, but at the same time I cannot admit that I was wrong, having been so impregnated with the, to me, nauseating smell and flavour of mildew. But I will admit this much, that Clos Fourtet often seems to possess naturally an aromatic, almost Oriental smell and a taste one might excusably connect with a drug-shop. The 1877 of that growth was a noteworthy example and an outstand-ingly fine wine, quite remarkable, and my friends in Bordeaux used to serve it in 1892 before, or with, or even after, a range of 1875s, when they were entertaining important guests from Great Britain or different parts of the Continent. One got to know it pretty well by heart and could hardly fail to recognize it, but the foreign *cognoscenti* were generally quite out of their depth when attempting to divine what it was. It must be something to do with the soil of St. Emilion because the early château bottling of 1923 Ch Cheval Blanc diffused that same strange Oriental aura that reminded my sensitive nostrils of the old Baker Street Bazaar of 1880! The early château bottling of the '23 Cheval Blanc, apart from its bouquet, recalled to my palate the sweetness and sunny savour of '75 more than any other wine I have recently tasted, but the later bottling was nothing like so good or so distinguishable. There is a moment for the best bottling of a wine. The same chord of pleasant memory was touched by a magnum of 1878 Ch Mouton Rothschild which we enjoyed at a luncheon party given to the Committee of the Saintsbury Club by Eddie Harvey (he who wore a straw hat summer and winter) and his partners. It took place in that historic 'Upper Room' of theirs, the erstwhile refectory of holy friars, in Denmark Street, Bristol. Alas! the glory and the beauty of it have departed, and the old building at this moment lies, like 25 Mark Lane, a mass of ruins, victim of another senseless Nazi airman, senseless because, savage-like, he wasted time and material in bombing civilians instead of military objectives. Horace Vachell was with us on the occasion and was enraptured with the 1878 Beychevelle, light and elegant, showing himself, as always, a born artist, and a connoisseur of beautiful things. The magnum of '78 Ch Mouton Rothschild which followed later was an altogether bigger and finer fellow, but it did not possess more sweet allure and daintiness than the Beychevelle. The members of the party on that occasion were Eddie Harvey, Jack Harvey, Charles Harvey, B Wright, André Simon, Horace Annesley Vachell, A J A Symons, Vyvyan Holland and myself. Between the two magnums of 1878, ie the Beychevelle and the Mouton Rothschild, Eddie was bold enough to give us a bottle of 1870 Ch Margaux which, after the rather extra-light Beychevelle, seemed, as I described it for *Wine and Food*, 'a giant, bearded like the pard, a little clumsy but good natured and sweet tempered, but it killed the gentle Beychevelle'.

Simon told me with great glee that the compositor had made the Margaux 'bearded like the padre' in his proof.

There are few more pleasant, cheering and, indeed, enlightening interludes in our lives than when a few men are gathered together who can drink and enjoy and discuss a good bottle (or two) of wine. One of the qualifications for the limited membership of the Saintsbury Club, founded, as is well known, in 1931, in honour of Professor George Saintsbury, is 'a love of wine and letters that is catholic and articulate', and I think that, speaking generally, men who possess this kind of double qualification are good mixers, good hearted, generous and artistic and what the Spaniards call *simpático*. This reminds me that it was at one of the earliest dinners of the Saintsbury Club that I heard the most eloquent dissertation on wine and letters to which it has ever been my privilege to listen. It was given by that most genial of literary scholars, Hilaire Belloc, and there is a keen feeling of disappointment among those who were present that night that we had no one there to take it down. I remember well that André Simon, our honorary cellarer, had given us an exceptionally good *impériale* (a bottle holding the equivalent of about eight or nine ordinary quart bottles) of 1878 Ch Latour, amongst other wines, and that Sir John Squire was in the chair. Belloc was smoking a big cigar when he rose and humorously remarked: 'Gentlemen, I am drunk. I have shared with you one of the finest bottles of claret I have ever tasted in my life.' He then proceeded to demonstrate in the choicest of language, rich in metaphor and quotation, without notes or manuscript, the close connection through the ages between wine and letters from the days of Aristotle to those of Saintsbury. It was a gem of erudition and oratory, and members of the new club were spellbound by it, an intellectual feast of which I suppose few if any of us have ever experienced the like. It is a great pity that the world has no verbatim report of it. Belloc also wrote some years ago a notable poem entitled 'Wine', and that brings to my mind another evening with the Saintsbury Club, on which the author of the poem himself occupied the chair. Duff Cooper, to whom, by the way, the poem was dedicated, came to the dinner from the House of Commons and was called upon for a speech. Now Duff Cooper is a fluent and witty impromptu speaker at any time, but he did not feel like it that evening after a no doubt hard day in the House. He was eventually persuaded, however, to get up and, after fumbling about for several seconds as if in search of a word, he said, 'I've forgotten the opening line of a poem and I ought not to have because it was dedicated to me'. Hilaire, quickly alive to the situation, quoted the first line of 'Wine', and Duff Cooper proceeded to recite with unerring sentiment and without any further hesitation the whole two hundred lines of the poem, a *tour de force* which won well-merited approbation and applause. One of my treasures is a proof-copy of the poem, with Hilaire Belloc's own corrections on it, which he himself was good enough to give me.

'Things' always go in 'threes', they say, and so I must, in passing, mention a third Saintsbury Club episode. I forget who occupied the chair on that particular occasion. We dine and wine in the picturesque fifteenth-century Court Room of the Vintners' Company – of which I am an exceedingly proud honorary Liveryman – and its superb carved-wood decorations, ornate, calm and mellow, must be the envy of all other City Companies and Guilds, particularly after their escape again, in the Battle of London in 1940–41 when so many of the other noble and time-honoured Halls were burnt to ashes or crumbled to dust. Our chairman has even had the privilege sometimes of occupying the Master's own beautifully adorned state chair, dated 1656, and of speaking with appropriate dignity and authority *ex cathedra*. On the right of the chair on this occasion was, I think, the late Baron de Cartier de Marchienne, the distinguished Belgian Ambassador, then *doyen du Corps Diplomatique,* one of the most genial and regular supporters of the Saintsbury Club and, like all good Belgians, a quick, sound judge of wines, particularly claret and burgundy. On the chairman's left, I know, was the Spanish Ambassador, Don Perez Ayala, *hombre muy simpático y amable,* a very observant, inquisitive and likeable personality, a novelist – he very kindly gave me a copy of one of his novels – and a good judge of *clarete* from which he claimed that the word claret derives. At the time of the Spanish Civil War he vanished, but I always hope we shall see him again. On his left was a great friend of mine, now dead I am sorry to say, who was an agent for a well-known cognac firm of brandy shippers. When at the close of dinner we came to the brandy, André Simon, the cellarer, gave us a *Fine Champagne* of 1900, a pale straw-coloured, clean, dryish liqueur of the kind much admired by the 'Trade' in recent years, but not yet sufficiently appreciated by the 'Public'. I sat next to my old friend and, leaning across him, Ayala, unwitting of his neighbour's connection with cognac, asked *me*, 'Why is this beautiful brandy so pale in colour?' My answer was that it had been shipped from France to this country when it was very young, about a year old, and been left in bond, untouched and unblended, until it was bottled about thirty years later. To my surprise my old friend intervened by saying, 'Ian, you are quite wrong', and, turning to Ayala, he added: 'This brandy is pale because the owner of it here has "racked" (transferred) it over and over again from cask to cask to prevent it from taking the colour of the wood'. I am sure my old friend believed that what he said was correct as he was a straight fellow, fonder, perhaps, of society than business, and was simply repeating what had been told him about other brandies. One has only to calculate, however, the cost as well as the loss of liquid that would be incurred by such frequent and perpetual 'racking' of brandy from cask to cask over a period of thirty years, to see what nonsense had been put into his mind. If the quality is fine and the vintage a good one, most of those who know prefer these pale 'unimproved' brandies for their own drinking. I certainly do, though I cannot criticize a public that has been educated to a more stereotyped and standardized article, carefully produced and not without attraction. Members of the wine and spirit trade should be very careful, I always think, to convey correct information to the layman, anxious for reliable facts, whose confidence and good will are always worth retaining.

If the amateur layman, except in the case of those who wish to display a knowledge which is non-existent, makes an error of fact or judgement, we in the trade ought to endeavour to dissipate any feelings of embarrassment by a frank and understanding correction. Sometimes, however, I am sorry to say there is a spice of mischievous satisfaction in administering a more caustic lesson to *poseurs* who know little but boast much. I remember that some years ago the Anglo-French Society in London gave a Luncheon of Honour to André Siegfried, the French historian, at the Savoy Hotel. Lord Stanley, I think, presided at the long head table which was adorned by illustrious personages of almost every calling in the social, diplomatic, literary and artistic world. The rest of the members and their guests were in the body of the hall, seated at round tables by their dozens or half dozens or other parts thereof, I found myself, as André Simon's guest, at a table of twelve between him and M Siegfried's lady secretary. Simon apparently was the 'host' for that table, as he turned to me and asked what wines he ought to order. I took a glance at the dozen inhabitants of the table and whispered, 'A bottle of ordinary red and a bottle of ordinary white and let them choose'. And it was so. I did not recognize that opposite Simon was one of the most polished of our journalists and most precise and omniscient of the Nation's mentors. During lunch, at the moment of a lull in the conversation, the mentor, who was drinking the red wine, placed two elegant fingers astride the stem of his wineglass which he pushed gracefully, almost sacrificially, towards André Simon with the words, *'Mais dites moi, Monsieur Simon, qu'est ce que c'est que ce vin* MERVEILLEUX?', strongly emphasizing the last word with the pose of a personal intelligence of anticipation. All the world waited for André's momentous pronouncement. His very quiet reply was *'Numéro un sur la liste du Savoy'*, and you could have heard the proverbial pin drop on the proverbial floor. We have chuckled over it often since. At the same time it was the circumstance that André Simon, the famous wine authority, well known as a connoisseur *par excellence,* was responsible for the wine's selection that misled the elegant journalist, as it might have any one of us, and it was only that assumption of his of superior knowledge and acumen that tickled impish mirth.

What a lot I owe to my lucky friendship with André Simon! Always ready to help and support, to advise, admonish and instruct, and to give of his best both materially and spiritually – he has been a true friend. In spite of long residence in this country and the fact that his dear wife is English, he has always remained a full-bodied and full-blooded Frenchman. He writes French and English equally well, although he tells me he finds it difficult to translate the full meaning of sentences and ideas from one language into the other. Many happy hours have we passed together, *inter alia inter pocula,* and, in good fortune and bad, in days of good repute and ill favour, of joy and sorrow, of success and failure, I have always found him a true, candid and sympathizing friend. May our journey together 'keep on to the end of the road'. No one who had the *entrée* to No 24 Mark Lane, when André was there with Fred and Percy Thellusson (successively Barons of Rendlesham) and enjoyed their hospitality 'during the luncheon hour', will ever forget those red-letter occasions. Although agents for Pommery, in those pre-1914 days the king of champagnes, this generous trio of wine experts and *bons vivants* did not confine their guest list to members of the wine trade, and one met at their table, soldiers and sailors, Peers of the Realm, Lords of Commerce, poets, peasants, artists and authors, all being regaled in princely fashion and educated to appreciate and enjoy the simplest of good English cooking associated with a meticulously selected range of wines and brandy. Both the Rendleshams learned their skill in wine from that superlatively sound and critical judge, Edward Burne, of the firm of Burne, Turner & Co, now woven into the Saccone & Speed group. Both were very quick in making up their minds, but Rendlesham the first was more reliable in his judgement than Rendlesham the second, though not quite so quick, nor quite so vehement, in giving it.

It was in that luncheon room when André Simon had around him John Squire, Guy Knowles, Maurice Healy, Earle Welby and A J A Symons, whose untimely death was an irreparable loss to English literature, that the decision was taken to found the Saintsbury Club in honour of the author of, amongst other no doubt more scholarly but not more popular volumes, *Notes on a Cellar-Book,* who was then well up in years. I was not present on that occasion, but they paid me the compliment of putting me on the original committee as a junior representative of wine, Simon 'the cellarer' being, of course, the senior.

It was in that room, too, that many schemes and publications, expeditions and adventures were discussed and launched for the benefit of mankind and, *sotto voce,* the wine trade. Simon, left alone as agent for Pommery by the retirement of the Rendlesham brothers, was, by his writings, lectures and entertaining, doing yeoman service in the interests of the trade, of which he was himself a pillar and an ornament, when pent-up troubles with the directors of the House at Reims suddenly exploded. When the dust and smoke of this bombshell had blown away, Pommery's agency was found to be in new hands and Simon, like the pilot, dropped. There were no two doubts that the name of Pommery had declined in public favour since the Great War in spite of the individual eminence of its representatives in this country, but, in my opinion, the fault lay in Reims and not in London. Beyond that I must not and do not care to pry, particularly as Simon retained the good will and regard of his numerous friends. It is also to André Simon that we owe the formation of the Wine and Food Society, which filled an aching void and immediately became a sure and even fashionable success. Soon A J A Symons came into it as Secretary and added a certain amount of quaintness and originality to its proceedings which no doubt have been duly recorded.

It is, however, entirely to Simon's spirit of enterprise that we are indebted for the Society's excellent quarterly. *Wine and Food,* to which many literary stars – not always planets, some indeed rather protoplasmic – have contributed articles dealing with solid or liquid aliments in a more or less unprofessional and light-hearted manner. Even I, unskilled wielder of the pen, have been a contributor on more than one occasion and suffered the horrors of Simon's blue pencil. I wrote the description of a special celebration in the late Ernest Cockburn's rather exotic new home in Oxted which had been but recently built to his order. My wife and I drove there with the Oldhams by car through the winding Surrey lanes, gloriously apparelled in rich autumn foliage, orange and scarlet and gold, with the gray, gauzy, ghost-like mist meandering eerily over our path. This contrasted with the warm spontaneity of the Cockburns' welcome to us; the brilliant illumination of their brightly carpeted halls; the well-cooked, substantial and savoury dinner, accompanied, needless to say, by a series of quite remarkable old wines; the dazzling glass, the lustrous silver and the gorgeous bowl in the centre of the table, filled with glowing aurora-tinted dahlias rejoicing in the romantic name of 'Peggy'. My story was itself a perfect, or nearly perfect, poem, and my dismay and disappointment can be imagined when the article appeared in *Wine and Food* shorn of all its delicate fantasy and beauty but correct in details of the menu, the *liste des vins* and the bowl of 'Peggy Wood' dahlias in the middle of the table. The blue pencil had been at work and I reproached André for cutting out the poetical part of my *chef d'œuvre*. His reply was short, pontifical and to the point: 'It may have been poetical but it wasn't gastronomical'. Here is the menu:

Turtle Soup
Dublin Bay Prawns
Sasarties (broiled beef fillets) with fried Pumpkin
Roast Pheasant
Chocolate Soufflé
Portuguese Tongue on Toast
Dessert

a pabulum which makes one's mouth water in 1945!
The accompanying Wines were:

Solera 1872 (bottled 1928)
Piesporter Goldtröpfchen 1935
Ch Latour 1899 (*magnum*)
Ch Léoville 1878 (*magnum*)
Ch Lafite 1870 (*bottled in Scotland*)
Krug 1928

Cockburn 1887
Cockburn 1858
Martell 1904
Hennessy 1906

As the dinner was in the autumn of 1938 it may be said that the 1887 Queen Victoria Jubilee Port was celebrating its own jubilee, and right royally did it do so. My notes say that the '78 Léoville, good though it was, could not compete with an excellent magnum of '99 Latour and the superb 1870 Lafite. The lucky diners were, besides, of course, Mr and Mrs Ernest Cockburn and my wife and myself, M and Madame André Simon, Mr and Mrs Eustace (Jerry) Oldham, Mrs Harold Cox, Barry Neame and Mr and Mrs Freddie Cockburn.

The 1870 Ch Margaux was a great wine, too, on a par with the Latour and Lafite and better than the Mouton Rothschild or any other 'growth'. It has not lasted quite so well as the Latour or Lafite which look, in 1945, as if they still have some years of a charmed existence to go. I get well chaffed as a rule when one of my friends serves a bottle of '70 as, this being of the year of my birth, I invariably remark that it has not yet reached its best. Nor have we, the '70s and I! Perfection still lies ahead! We shall never attain it though we ever conscientiously pursue it. When can you say a wine reaches its best? There cannot be a hard and fast rule. Some 1929 vintage wines are already almost *passés*: Lafite 1870 on the other hand is alive, very much alive. Vintages vary; bottles vary; wines of the same vintage do not always maintain a uniform stamina. That is an obvious generality applicable *mutatis mutandis* to many forms of organic life, but I doubt if a more precise answer to the question is possible. When does a man reach his best? Or a tree? A period of years may show little or no difference, no definite progress, no definite decline; qualities of strength, beauty and energy may remain apparently static for an indefinite time. Only a wine that has been made from unripened, rotten or defective grapes, or a wine lacking in essential constituents, such as sugar or tannin, or a wine whose foul smell connotes impurity or disease, can be quickly condemned in its early stages, as these are faults from which it will not recover. Lightness of body does not necessarily indicate poorness of quality or a fatal lack of stamina – often quite the contrary; but it may, and often does, although not always, portend early maturity and inability to 'make old bones'. 1871, 1877, 1905 and 1923 might perhaps represent good light vintages of comparatively early decline, and 1864, 1875 and 1900 of the converse; for all these three lived to a healthy old age. Contrariwise, great fullness of body does not guarantee excellence of quality; it may indeed conceal coarseness, excess of tannin, hardness and a lack of sugar (not always) that will never be overcome, though it may take many years to confirm these failings. 1844, 1887, 1890 and 1918 would be examples of inability to grow old agreeably, and 1865, 1868, 1870 and 1906, which eventually threw off their tannin mask, the exceptions. There is one sure axiom that never fails. If a wine is bad or unsound when it is young, it will never be good however long it may be kept. While on the subject I like to recall a famous Jeroboam of '70 Margaux I got from Cockburn & Campbell and, after a lengthy rest, served, at No. 25 Mark Lane, to a small party of trade experts the list of whose names was destroyed in the blitz. It was only an office lunch, and I could not make up my mind what to give my guests in front of the old '70 as, by precept and experience, something ought to precede and lead up to it. I had one of those brainwaves dear to the heart of the unorthodox and enterprising wine student and determined to give the party the youngest Château Margaux I had, and the oldest, introducing them, as it were, to each other. Thus it was that I served the 1929, a young, fresh, full in the mouth, sweet, most promising child of a somewhat dangerous vintage, and it fell into its place in a marvellous manner by being modest and pleasant itself and showing off its old kinsman to the greatest advantage. The empty jeroboam, with the tricolour ribbon still round its neck, stands, or stood till recently, in the office of Messrs Corney & Barrow, whose director, Charles Stevens – 'Uncle Charles' as he is affectionately nicknamed – was one of my guests on the occasion. Commander Tuffill, the old-world-courtesy clerk of the Vintners' Company, who was also of the party, wrote me a few days later about the '70: 'What a charm and memory of our forefathers!' Both he and I were born in '70. Forefathers indeed! In 1945 we are still drinking first growths of 1870 and still marvelling at the volume of life and sugar that lurks in their deep brown depths.

When I was in Bordeaux in 1892 I became quite romantically attached to Ch Margaux: its wines were to me the *beau-ideal* of claret, and I enjoyed the good fortune, either then or in subsequent years, of proving the well-bred elegance and subtlety of their bouquet and flavour over many famous vintages from 1847 onwards. The '47 Margaux I starred as 'magnificent' after Clicquot '75 and '75 Rauzan and Brane-Cantenac. Ten days earlier I had had the '47 and '48 Lafite 'both rather fine', and six weeks later I had '47 Palmer, Rauzan and Haut-Brion and notch the last named as *'exquis'*. Whether *'exquis'* surpasses 'magnificent' I am not sure. Alas! Ch Margaux, in the opinion of most of us, is no longer what it was, and has not been since it gave us the winsome 1900. Whether the enlargement of its vineyard and erection of more capacious *chais,* in which to house the increased harvest of wine, has resulted in over-production and some loss of concentrated individuality is a question that is giving many claret lovers besides myself furiously to think. If that is the only cause of a generally admitted decline in estimation we need not be worried as the remedy is probably already being put into operation, and Château Margaux may be expected to shine once again in the constellation of great stars. Amen.

What a contrast the 1870s are to the 1875s which were certainly passing their apogee some forty years ago, though Berry Bros and Rudd even today (August 1945) seem to have a bottle or two left of 1875 Ch Palmer which retains much of the native charm and honeyed sunshine that characterized that vintage in its best days. Another 'memorable bottle', as André Simon might say, that I enjoyed the privilege of 'putting up' was an *impériale,* or jeroboam, of 1864 Ch Lafite. I had joined Barry Neame, the well-known managing director of the Hind's Head Hotel at Bray-on-Thames and builder of its fame, in the purchase of three *impériales* of this most famous, to the passing generation, of all clarets. He took one himself, I think Simon took another, and I took the third. In its honour I 'threw' a small dinner party at the Hind's Head. Barry put up a grand dinner and the Lafite, decanted by Simon and myself, nobly played the part of the hero. Graceful, brilliant, generous, majestic even in the fading twilight of declining years, the wine was still an outstanding triumph of the Bordeaux vineyards. We toasted George Atkinson who was also a 'sixtyfourian' and proud of it and, with his steadfast quality, dignified demeanour and generous nature, a worthy son of what he and we looked upon as a famous vintage.

MENU OF DINNER, 7th JUNE 1938
TO MEET
A JEROBOAM OF 1864 CHATEAU LAFITE
(health permitting)
And other old Bordeaux Friends

*

On Arrival
KRUG 1928 (*in Magnums*)

*

THE DINNER

1920 Domaine de Chevalier	Giblet Soup
(*Magnum*)	Savoury Eggs
1899 Château Latour	Saddle of Mutton
(*Magnum*)	Worthing Beans
	Braised Onions
	New Potatoes
1864 Château Lafite (*Jeroboam*)	Creamed Mushrooms
	Asparagus
	Cheese Soufflé
'*A Humble Offering*'	
Hine's 1904 (*bonded* 1905)	Strawberries and Cream
	Coffee

Present at the Dinner, besides my wife and myself, were:

M and Madame André L Simon
Mr Eustace and Lady Peggy Hoare

45

Mr and Mrs George D Atkinson
Mr E A S (Jerry) and Mrs Oldham
Mr and Mrs Lorne Campbell
Barry Neame
Curtis Moffat
Maurice Healy
and
A J A Symons

To Barry Neame be the entire credit for the most excellent dinner menu, in perfect harmony with the trio of clarets which it was chosen to accompany.

When he opened his own *impériale*, Barry provided an equally well-chosen dinner and a longer panel of wines. I may mention that it is only in recent years that I have heard the name *impériale* applied to a bottle of wine. Jeroboam and Rehoboam, those two wicked kings respectively of Israel and Judah, always quarrelled with each other, and the presumptuous claim of each of them to have out-size bottles of wine called after him is still a source of heated and often acrimonious discussion. Nebuchadnezzar and Methuselah seem also to have butted in with claims of their own. The United Nations Organisation should be involved at once to settle this at least two thousand nine hundred year old dispute. I suggest that the way out of this bottleneck is to simplify bottle nomenclature. A MAGNUM we know is a two-bottle bottle and a DOUBLE-MAGNUM a four-bottle bottle; let a TRIPLE-MAGNUM be a six-bottle bottle and, discarding once and for all those two unworthy reprobates, Jeroboam and Rehoboam, let us adopt the noble name 'IMPÉRIALE' for the eight- (sometimes nine-) bottle bottle.

BARRY'S DINNER
On Arrival

	Krug 1928	Appetizers
		(*NB* – He would not
		call them *hors d'œuvre*)

AT DINNER

	Sherry, Amontillado Pasado	Melon
	(Duff Gordon)	
1937	Neidermenniger Herrenberg	Lobster Mould
	Spätlese	
1923	Dom de Chevalier (*Magnum*)	Saddle of Mutton
		H H H Garden Peas
1899	Château Latour (*Magnum*)	Worthing Beans
		New Potatoes
1878	Ch Léoville-Poyferré (*Magnum*)	
1864	Château Lafite (*Impériale*)	Cheese Soufflé
1870	Château Lafite (*additional*)	
1900	Cockburn, Vintage Port	Nectarines and Peaches
1900	Hine's Grande Fine	Coffee
	Champagne (*landed* 1901)	

The '64 had not decanted so well as it had done on the occasion of my little dinner, but, in topical parlance, it drank very well.

Amongst those present on this memorable occasion were the late Ernest Cockburn, Israel Sieff, Hastings Perkin, Eustace Hoare, Douglas West, Dick Godson, Monty Dobson, Stanley de Ville, André Simon and one or two others, As was his custom, Barry asked us all to place the clarets in order of merit on cards he gave us. This, although amusing and an incentive perhaps to careful tasting, was of course an absurd game, since to compare the respective merits of, say, a fine 1858 claret and a fine 1928 claret would be impossible. It would be like the effort sometimes made to decide whether Grace, or Trumper, or Hobbs, or Bradman was the greatest batsman. Nevertheless we all played, and my card read: 1st, 1864 Lafite; 2nd, 1870 Lafite; 3rd, 1923 Chevalier; 4th, 1899 Latour; and 5th, 1878 Léoville, which indicated pretty clearly that, in my opinion, the Latour and Léoville were not up to their own usual standard: they ought both to have beaten the gallant Chevalier. It is not uninteresting to note, however, that the final consensus of lists confirmed my own except that the '70 Lafite was defeated by the Chevalier for second place! The '64 romped home an easy winner: a worthy farewell to a time-honoured champion.

CHAPTER 4

Class Distinctions in the Vineyards

Classification. Wine Trade Club. 1899 and 1900 Clarets. '77 Cheval Blanc and its Corks. John Burns. Ausone.

Although I prefer 1875 as a vintage for all-round excellence, it did not in my opinion produce any one wine to equal the 1864 Lafite – the finest claret I ever drank. Sixty leading clarets of the Médoc, which was the 'Belgravia' of the Bordeaux vineyard in the year of grace 1855, were authoritatively classified in that year into five groups under the name of first, second, third, fourth and fifth *crus classés,* or 'classed growths' as we call them. That was nearly a hundred years ago and the classification has well stood the test of time. As Belgravia was the exclusive hub of the aristocracy so, with the exception of one Graves wine, the Ch Haut-Brion, no other wines than those of the Médoc were included in the circle of the *élite. La classification* was the Debrett of Bordeaux. Nowadays the *Vignoble de Bordeaux,* like most of the world's most cherished institutions, has taken a distinct turn to the Left, and the social position not only of Graves wines but also that of the still more democratic wines of St. Emilion would have to be taken into account in any reclassification. Even in the Médoc itself there are growths unclassified, except collectively as *'bourgeois'* and *'artisans'* – the upper and lower middle classes,

49

many of which are only 'a little lower than the angels'. Roses and
lilies are not the sole denizens of the floral world: there are also
daisies and buttercups of unsurpassable beauty in their proper
places; but, for the adornment of your drawing-room you use
roses and lilies not buttercups and daisies, and similarly you
serve the 'classed growths' of claret at your dinner-table and not
the humbler, though often worthy, *'bourgeois'* and *'artisans'*. The
bourgeois may not stay so well but, when at their best, they are
strong candidates for places among the Seats of the Mighty. The
Ch Citran, for instance, and the Ch Pomys, the Ch d'Angludet,
Chasse-Spleen, Pontac-Lynch, Priban, Lanessan, Martinens,
Trois-Moulins, so popular in Holland, the land of windmills,
these and many others, in their good years, are at least equal to
some of the fifth classed growths or even fourth. Nor, as I have
insisted, can the old aristocratic Châteaux of the Médoc expect
much longer to enjoy their favoured position. Their owners'
praiseworthy example of concentrated care upon their vineyards
and their wines, of jealous pride in their good name, honourable
career and proprietary responsibilities, has been followed by the
vine-growers of the Graves and the Saint Emilionnais. In both
these districts, honeycombed with beautifully kept vineyards,
wines are produced rivalling those of the Médoc and in many
years surpassing all but the best. Ch Haut-Brion has now, it is
rumoured, I hope falsely, absorbed the vineyard of La Mission
across the road, but this latter sent out of its *chais* – *for* the enjoyment of man, and under the name of La Mission-Haut-Brion
– wines that could compare with those from its great neighbour who was admitted in 1855 to honorary membership of
the Médocain classification as a Premier Cru and, up to twenty
years or so ago, had fully merited the compliment. The 1905

La Mission-Haut-Brion reached a pitch of excellence equalled in my opinion by no other wine of the vintage, not even the Haut-Brion itself, good though this latter was in spite of its blotting-paper colour and *goût d'orange*. André Simon, Francis Berry and I found a magnum of La Mission '05 at the Trocadero in the autumn of its days. It figures in the photograph of the three of us that appeared on the dust cover of Andre's *Tables of Content*. It is to be found no longer anywhere that I know of, and the magnums soon disappeared from J Lyons & Company's List! Whither? Ah!

Other Graves wines that would apply for classification would include the Haut-Brion-Larrivet, the Smith-Haut-Lafitte, the Haut-Bailly (the Pape-Clément has, I believe, gone out of cultivation), possibly, if big enough, the Malartic-Lagravière and, certainly, the Domaine de Chevalier, one of my own favourite growths. Its wines are generally light and perhaps lacking in volume of bouquet, but they are always made with the utmost care by a proud and skilful owner, and, even in years distinctly poor elsewhere, you will often find a little gem at Chevalier. I remember, when the Wine Trade Club was domiciled in that 'flat-iron' building at the corner of Great Tower Street and Byward Street which I had the pleasure of 'Opening' on 29 January 1913, during my year of Presidency, and which building was resold after the First Great War and blitzed to smithereens in the Second, that the proprietor of Chevalier visited the Club and, later, sent us a gift of two bottles each of six successive vintages – and they were all good, very good. We had a unique wine-list in the dining-room during the brief sojourn of the Club in that building, a list of treasures and curiosities, including a beautiful Ruwer wine from Deinhard which I specially recall as my colleagues on the committee used to be amused to hear my struggles with Eitelsbacher Karthäuserhofberg of 1908, a clean, light, sharp, flavoury wine, ideal for a luncheon party, of which we had many. The Ruwer, I should mention, is a tributary of the Moselle. We had some happy days there before Kaiser Wilhelm thought to win world dominion in 1914 and opened an era of wars and rumours of wars, now happily closed in August 1945. One day, I remember, several champagne agents each brought a bottle of their 1892 vintages, admirable all. The competition was very keen and the tasting very enjoyable. If memory serves me well Dry Monopole was acclaimed the winner.

The most popular claret at the club for a long time was the 1899 Ch La Lagune, shipped by Johnston and not château-bottled, a luscious, velvety, virile wine that went down as the saying is, like hot rolls. Many were the discissions and tastings we had to decide upon the respective merits of the 1899 and 1900 claret vintages and unanimity was never reached. Both were fine, 1899 fuller in body, more vigorous, sweet and generous with a slightly annoying aftertaste of grape stalks, as if the stalks had been left with the grapes in their pressing: this gradually disappeared with age. The 1900s, on the other hand, were light, very light, in body, but just as sweet as 1899 and soft and gentle, almost too much so to age well. But many have safely passed their fortieth birthday and have grown in body, and today, I find, have tasted if anything rather better than their great rivals. The two vintages, grown old together side by side, were always the fine gentleman and his gracious lady; Darby and Joan indeed; may they be preserved to us for still a little longer.

I am afraid the Chevalier has taken me away from the subject of reclassification. All those Graves wines that I have mentioned might find a place on a new list, and there may be others; and, although the St Emilionnais has been termed earthy and common and more like burgundy than claret, there are no doubt several 'growths' there that have so improved their culture that they must be included in any list that admits other than Médoc wines. Most lovers of claret will place Ch Ausone and Ch Cheval Blanc in the same category as second growths of the Médoc, and in some years on an equality with the first growths. Who that remembers the 1877 Ch Cheval Blanc which they drank at the old Café Royal would place it second to any but the top growths of that year? If it had only been better corked – the Café was not to blame – it might be still drinkable. Why do niggardly bottlers of wine use second-rate corks which so often destroy whole bins of good wine and drive would-be wine devotees on to beer and spirits? What false economy! I remember a wine merchant who had to uncork and recork nearly all his young vintage port of a certain year because the people who bottled it for him had used what we call short corks, and poor ones at that, and the wine oozed out. The expense of the operation was far heavier than the extra cost of long and fine corks would have been, and the quality of the wine must have suffered. Wine is worthy of every care during the whole course of its career.

Ch Cheval Blanc 1875 was also very fine, and, to come to more recent years, I have already alluded to the 1921 and 1923 and I might add the 1906, very sweet and full in the mouth, and the 1926 which was an outstanding success in what I consider to be, up to date, a much underrated claret vintage; a little coarse and hard, perhaps, but not lacking in sugar, and likely still to develop gentility.

Ch Ausone has always been rather a mystery to me: although from its name its vineyard must have produced wine for many centuries, it is only in comparatively recent years that it has come to the front. I have no record in my storehouse of memories of ever hearing it mentioned, nor of visiting the *Château,* during my sojourn in Bordeaux in 1892 and 1893, but St Emilion wines were not fashionable then, and almost taboo at dinner parties. One calls to mind the story of the Cabinet Minister's wife and Mrs John Burns, and remembers how far apart were Belgravia and Battersea in the old days. The story, and it is only a story, will perhaps bear repeating. When John Burns of Battersea, that stalwart British working-man who boasted a catholic taste in books and an aptitude for politics as well as cricket (as I know from having played with him), became a member of Campbell-Bannerman's Cabinet in 1906, the story goes that the wife of one of his colleagues in the Cabinet did not call on Mrs Burns. When, however, she and her husband gave one of the big political receptions, which were so important a feature of those days, she wrote a polite letter to Mrs Burns excusing herself for not having called on account of the distance of Belgravia from Battersea and hoping Mr and Mrs Burns would waive ceremony and accept an invitation to the party. Mrs Burns is said to have replied that, as Battersea was just as far from Belgravia as Belgravia was from Battersea, she much regretted that she and Mr Burns were unable to accept the kind invitation. Belgravia and Battersea are undoubtedly nearer today!

I suppose that the wines of Ausone were being drunk in some quarters in those days even if they did not come my way, and the '71, '74, '75, and '77 and '78 may have been excellent specimens of those famous years – what a wonderful triumphal decade claret then enjoyed! – but I never heard of them. Possibly the quantity then made in each year was so small that but few people ever obtained any: now the fear is that the extension of the vineyard and its big production may become a danger to its growing popularity. In Simon's old office, No 24 Mark Lane (next door to us at No. 25), we several times compared at luncheon the Ch Ausone of 1904 and 1905. Both were very pleasing and attractive: the latter was the lighter in body, but very soft and silky, and, with my undisguisable bias towards 1905, I think I generally gave it best though the 1904 was much more smooth and supple than were the majority of wines of that vintage. When 1904s first came on the market after the cheap, thin and hungry, but commercially useful, wines of 1901, 1902 and 1903, they looked like giants, and people rashly talked of '90s and '87s, but they were not really very heavy and, with a little more sugar and a little less steel, they might have developed into acceptable wines, just as their natural successors, the 1906 and 1911, did. Ch Ausone would, on its present reputation, occupy a high place in a new classification and the 1934 is well worth while watching. Both it and the Cheval Blanc, I understand, extend their vineyards over the patches of gravelly soil that have found their way into St. Emilion. I am not sure if this is so and if the Clos Fourtet, which is on the site of an old camp, is on exactly similar soil, but, in spite of its peculiar aromatic flavour, it certainly ought also to find a place in any list of the new *élite*. Railway porters now become governors of Indian Provinces and good luck to them! *Tempora mutantur,* let us hope *pro bono public*!

There are Canons and Saints and other kinsfolk of St Emilion entitled, perhaps, to recognition of some sort, but they are rather split up amongst themselves and distinction might be invidious. St. Emilionnais as a matter of fact have their own classification and, as far as I can see, every vineyard is a *premier cru classé*. Nor could the claims of Pomerol be overlooked. The Conseillante, Petrus, L'Evangile and Certan are all in the running, but the wines of this district, though most attractive and admirable when young, ought really to be drunk at that stage because they rarely if ever age satisfactorily.

I have said enough, however, about the reclassification which is being demanded in certain quarters. It is really a matter for the Bordeaux people themselves and, beyond suggesting, with all due deference, that Mouton Rothschild should be added to the four first growths, I would be content to leave the list as it stands, anyhow until the many projected fusions, closing-downs and disappearances now under consideration have been effected. The whole world has altered in aspect and outlook as a result of the two great Wars, and (I write this in August 1945) the recent capture of the elusive nuclear atom, and the harnessing of its power for the service of mankind, will involve changes so revolutionary in character and so incalculable that all our standards of living and all our mundane interests and activities will have to be modified and remodelled to meet the new and, let us hope, better conditions that now loom, brilliant and enticing, though a little awesome, on the horizon. Yes: the reclassification of claret growths can, perhaps, wait.

CHAPTER 5

Tales of Testing and Tasting

On Tasting Wine. The Four Essays. '58 Lafite. '63 Rebello Valente.
'75 Clarets in 1892 and 1893. Sweetness in Claret. 1887 *et seq.* Arthur
Southard. Maurice Healy. La Lagune. Drinking Wines Young. Reading
Grantham and a Dinner Party. '68 Cockburn. 1908 Ports Competition.
Revenons à nos Moutons. Mardi Gras.

I acclaim the 'seventies as a wonderful decade while I am still
dealing with Bordeaux, whose wines are the wines of the true
wine lover. My advice to anybody who wishes to become a good
judge of all kinds of wines is to start with the study of claret – a
wine of infinite variety which age cannot wither nor custom
stale. An intimate knowledge of so simple and natural a wine
as claret is the best foundation for acquiring a knowledge of all
wines. *Veni vidi vici* has been looked upon as a soldierly and
inspiring alliterative epigram in matters military, and there is
no reason why we should not introduce an epigram equally
apt and instructive in the case of wine. How would this do:
'See, smell, sip, swallow'? First you raise your glass to *see* the
wine's colour and condition, next you *smell* the wine to satisfy
yourself that it is clean and correct, then you *sip* it to confirm
or contradict your sense of smell and, finally, you *swallow* it
for compensation, comfort and contentment. An easy play on

the letter *s* would convert this ritual into 'The Four Essays in Wine'. Then, as I mentioned earlier, you must try to remember the accumulated outcome of your investigation: soon you will be having a guess at the vintage year and perhaps even at the 'growth'. Myself when young used to find this guessing at vintage and growth much easier than I do today, and I have, in my time, had moments both of gratification and shame as memory and judgement have played me either fair or false. The older vintages seem to me to have preserved more individuality of character than do the modern vintages which, with more uniformity, are less distinguishable. It may be, on the other hand, that my own palate is at fault, not so sensitive as it was and not so finely tuned to the organs of memory which also may be getting rusty. There is, without question, great satisfaction in knowing what you are drinking, and, in suitable company, your host will always tell you. In Bordeaux the *sommelier,* or wine butler, announced each wine as he filled one's glass. When you look at a picture you may hazard the name of the painter but you like to have your conjecture verified, and the same satisfaction is demanded when you hear music and are not sure whether you have recognized the right composer or not. My advice about wine is always to have a shot at what it is, even if, for fear of disclosing an error, you keep your fancy to yourself. It is one of the ways that will teach you to be a good taster, and you need never apologize for making a mistake. The best connoisseurs often do. There are as many reasons against infallibility as there are against prophesying the winner of the Grand National. But it seems to me that, in the old days, one could almost always make sure of spotting an 1858, or 1864, or an 1875 and other wines of the pre-phylloxera period: the phylloxera indeed may itself have robbed the vines of the power to impart a strong touch of personality to their product.

Talking of 1858 reminds me of the Lafite of that year for which, when I was comparatively young in the trade, and it was very much younger than it is today, I acquired a great partiality. I am going astern forty or fifty years and bringing back to mind my then senior partner, Nevile Reid, father of the Nevile who went with me to Dijon and grandfather of the Nevile who is now my partner. He was severe in business but most generous and hospitable outside, with a fund of good stories and a fountain of quotations from the Psalms (which I think he knew off by heart) through Shakespeare and Milton and most of our leading poets. He often had me down to his house in Hanworth where he lived next door to George Pollock the Remembrancer. It was there, at 'The Oaks', that I learnt to appreciate the 1858 Ch Lafite, a fine, elegant, sweet, flavoury claret, then at its zenith or just peeping over the top of the hill. It had been hard and stubborn in its youth but eventually came into its own and won the admiration of the experts. Reid senior and I must have emptied quite a number of bottles together as Mrs Reid was no competitor and the family was as often as not also onlooking rather than partaking. They preferred champagne, I think, and, as their parents entertained a good deal, they had excellent reason to leave their father and me to enjoy our claret. This is where my distressing story comes in. There was a big dinner party at 'The Oaks', at which I was one of the guests: smart men, beautiful women, frills and *frou-frou*, elegant illumination, glass, silver and flowers making a brilliant scene such as that genius for word-colour, Alphonse Daudet, would have loved to describe. Champagne, in meritorious plenty, was served during dinner and, at dessert, 'claret or port'. Having enjoyed my champagne I felt claret would be out of place and took port like everybody else. A topping, good, gay and most enjoyable party, but next morning the fury of Father Reid burst like a bombshell upon me. He had decanted a bottle of the '58 Lafite expressly for me and I had left it untouched! A folly! A discourtesy!! A crime!!! He was very hurt, and though, with sincere sympathy for his disappointment – and my own – I tried to explain that I was given no choice when the 'Krug' went round and had felt that port was the proper follow to that, he was somehow not convinced that the fault of neglect was not mine. I often used to wonder afterwards what I would have done had I been offered during the dinner 'champagne or claret'? I hope and believe I would have said 'claret': anyhow, I emptied the decanter next day, contrary to all expert convention, and the wine was still wonderfully good: a great wine that '58 Lafite, 'worthy progenitor' of the '64.

I remember another evening at 'The Oaks', again after a decanter of the '58 had been discussed to our mutual satisfaction. My good host and I faced a decanter of port when the ladies had retired to the drawing-room. 'Ian,' said he, 'I want you to taste this port which I always think is the best ever made.' I said I would be very glad to and, having helped myself to a glass, I passed the decanter towards him and was about to pour him out one. 'No, Ian,' said he, 'I must not. I should suffer fearful heartburn in the night.' I expressed my regret and began to enjoy the colour and bouquet and first sip of a wine which was exquisite. I asked what it was and learnt that it was 1863 Rebello Valente. What with talking (on his part) and sipping (on mine), the glass was not long in becoming empty and louder grew my praises of its flavour, its fruit and its charm. 'Have another glass, Ian', said my envious host. I say envious because I had little difficulty in persuading him to join me with my second glass, and I am not sure that his entertaining conversation did not give me time to enjoy a third before we retired to our respective apartments. We met again next morning, and my first words to him were, 'Well, how did you sleep last night?' 'A night of torture,' was his grim reply, 'I hardly slept a wink.' Since I became an elderly man myself and have suffered similar uneasiness and discomfort, not necessarily only after port, I can sympathize with him more now than I was able to do at the time. I can only hope he took the philosophic view I have sometimes done myself and murmured meditatively when morning brought relief: 'It was worth it'.

I doubt if anybody living today, except perhaps my old friend, Jean Calvet,[1] of Bordeaux and that splendid taster and critic, Hastings Perkin, can have enjoyed such opportunities as I had of seeing and sampling the 1875 clarets at their very best in 1892 and 1893. They were inordinately light, sweet and precocious, alluring and irresistible, with the sword of Damocles hovering over them from birth, but happily deferring its expected fall for many years. In Bordeaux they were being served as the *bonne bouche* at dinner parties as early as the autumn of 1884, as I saw from an old menu which was shown to me by Robert Cunningham, at that time a younger member of the then important City firm of Forbes, Cunningham and Bond, absorbed at a later date by the even greater firm of Portal,

---

[1] M Jean Calvet passed very peacefully away in the Spring of 1946.

Dingwall and Norris. It was not a question of drinking them only on ceremonial or festive occasions. Though much prized, they were almost the daily beverage: people were so afraid of their collapse.

> 'This thought is as a death, which cannot choose
> But weep to have that which it fears to lose.'

The shrewd Bordelais, however, did not waste time in weeping and took the most appropriate measures to ensure that their loss should be minimized as far as possible. But what an experience for young fellows out there at the time, like the late Walter Berry and myself who were *en pension* together, and others equally keen to learn in so agreeable a school! To gauge the intrinsic worth of anything it is well to be able to compare it with the best possible of its kind. It may add a little severity to your judgement, and, if you are crankish, it may make you finicky, but it will add much to the value of your criticism, condemnation or praise. I shall always owe a debt of gratitude to the scores of bottles of 1875 claret I shared and enjoyed in Bordeaux in 1892 and 1893 and the many kind friends who were good enough to provide them and encourage my desire for education: no one could have been luckier.

One of the outstanding characteristics of the '75s was their extraordinary sweetness. We never seem to see it in the clarets of nowadays and it is one of the first attributes I look for. You will still find it, or remember it, in the older vintages such as '58, and '64, '65 and '68, '70, '71, '74, '75 and '77 and, to a lesser degree, in '78, but thereafter one almost looks for it in vain in most vintages. Some of the wines of the 'eighty decade displayed a mawkish sweetness which was the camouflage of mildew and unpalatable. But the 1880 Mouton Rothschild was a notable exception and turned out really well, with a good deal of the flavour and sweetness of the earlier decade. I have drunk it with pleasure as recently as 1945 at Charles Hasslacher's hospitable luncheon-table in Idol Lane. It looked as though the official regulations governing the spraying of sugar on the must at the time of vintage, to promote fermentation, had in these poor years been disregarded and early decay promoted instead.

The 1887, full-blooded, indeed, was hard and dry but started a sort of recovery – short-lived it is true. 1888 gave early promise of charm and sweetness, but the talons of mildew were remorseless. 1889, a miniature '88, shared its fate. 1890, like '87, was, and still is, as hard and dry as wood. 1891 and 1896 both lacked sugar or, with their style and flavour, might have made a better name for themselves. There was a Ch Laroque of St Emilion 1891, of which Schröder and Schÿler bought the whole crop, which was light and sweet and most attractive. I became quite enamoured of it, and the firm backed me up, the partners even laying down a few dozens in their own private cellars; but from that day to this I never heard another word about it and have often wondered why. There was none left when I wanted some for England. That rapid disappearance of wines, just as noticeable today as it was in the case of the 1891 Laroque, is one of the mysteries of the Bordeaux trade and, I think, can only be explained by the enormous consumption of wine in France itself. It is little known in this country that France is not only the largest exporter of wine but also the largest importer. No wonder the French are an unconquerable people.

Even truth, as well as Gallic humour, can be funny and mis-
leading sometimes. We in the trade were highly amused when,
after the liberation of France towards the end of the war, we
obtained permission from the Ministry of Food to renew contact with our Bordeaux friends and negotiate a purchase from
them of cheap claret. When we attempted to do this, however,
we were met with the astonishing reply, 'We cannot sell you any
cheap claret because we are not allowed to import any wine from
Algeria!' In view of the time-honoured suspicion, entertained
by some members of the public, that blending of Bordeaux and
Algerian wines for this market is a common practice, this excuse
seemed damning indeed, but it was, as it happened, the correct and only one. The French people must have their *ordinaire*
for daily consumption, and the Bordeaux merchants, prevented
by war restriction on shipping from meeting the demand, as
they always did in the past, with imported Algerian wine, had
perforce to do so from their own stocks, leaving them little else
than their finer wines when we came along with our demands:
but the protest coming from Bordeaux itself gave us all a good
laugh. The wartime quota of Algerian wine was an unexpected
godsend. Though crude and coarse it made a refreshing drink
when diluted with a thimbleful of water, and, if it did little else,
it rekindled a yearning for the touch, on our lips, of vanished
wines and the sound of names that, for the time being, were still.

To avoid being as dry as many of the vintages I mention I
shall just glide chronologically over them. I come then to two
years, 1892 and 1893, in which there was, without question,
sugar of a sort, but, in '92, it was burnt sugar and destroyed its
host as the moth destroys the garment in which it nests, and
in '93, a fine, big, supple wine, the sugar was tempered by a

soupçon of acidity which just prevented the vintage from being in the front rank of the famous: many '93s are still very drinkable. Arthur Southard, winebroker, auctioneer, connoisseur, and patron of the turf, discovered and exaggerated the squeeze of lemon in the wine's 'farewell' and slated vintage '93 up hill and down dale. He carried his intolerance of it to extremes and bought largely of 1894, pretty, but of poor quality, which he declared to be a much better year. He was wrong just as he had been some twenty years earlier when he went in heavily for 1876, saying that its wines were of finer quality than those of 1875. These preferences, I think, were due more to temperament than conviction as he was an excellent judge of wine and became celebrated as one of the chief figures in the Burnay Port Sale. His sunburnt face and grey topper were well known in the City: how strange it is to recall that we all, *de rigueur*, wore top hats in those days; but few aspired to the courtly grey.

The 1895s were fat and flabby but most of them certainly contained a good amount of what one might call evanescent sugar, some, indeed, too much to save them from a, perhaps, premature eclipse. The Lafite and Mouton Rothschild, however, excelled, and the Conseillante, Pomerol, was extraordinarily good. When I saw them at their respective châteaux in, I suppose, 1897, I found the Mouton superb and asked Albert Schÿler to buy some and let me take a few dozen for my own very juvenile cellar. It was only some ten years ago that, at Elm Grove, Ockham, I opened the last bottle to prove to Maurice Healy and André Simon that it was better than the Lafite of the same year, of which André had kindly sent me a bottle or two. Unluckily the bottle which we opened of the Lafite was far from showing well and the Mouton on that occasion took the palm.

It had one great blemish: it always tasted as if the sediment had at some time or other gone through it. The competition was a convenient excuse for a happy meeting. Poor Maurice, whose lonely suffering made one feel that death was a relief, used to come down to Ockham to see a sick friend: he was a charming companion, the essence of kindness, with a quick innate Irish wit and a merry, betimes sanctimonious, tongue. He was an obstinate advocate but not always a reliable guide in his choice of wines: he worked hard to acquire knowledge, an effort that was thwarted by his quaint fancies such as the terrible 1910 Ch Haut-Brion, of which he was clever enough to talk his friends into a false and unmerited admiration. His book, *Stay me with Flagons*, was an instant success, well-worth reading on literary grounds alone, and is often quoted to me as a sort of winelovers' *vade mecum*. About the 1896 vintage, elegant but cold, I have little more to say than that a little sugar in it might have given it a place with the immortals.

We can dismiss 1897 and 1898 as undistinguished and come to the only two vintages of claret since the invasion of the phylloxera that have proved themselves to be in the very front rank, the 1899 and the 1900. I have described earlier in these pages the controversy that has always raged between their respective admirers, and we may be thankful that occasionally, for instance as guests of C M Wells or Eustace Hoare, we still have an opportunity of comparing their rival merits. They are both growing old gracefully and gradually but are horribly scarce.

Nothing outstanding in the way of sweetness characterized 1901, '02, '03 and '04, to which I have previously alluded, and even 1905s, which were great favourites of mine and many of which were in their way sweet, never contained or showed the sunny sweetness that made the '75s so popular in Great Britain, for many years a happy claret-drinking country in consequence. Bordeaux people always think we want big, heavy, beefy clarets, but they are wrong: light wines, with ample sugar and fine flavour, are those we most admire, though we certainly do not favour miserably thin dreary things like 1882, 1897, 1910 and 1930, even admitting in them a modicum of sugar and flavour.

The 1906 was one of the beefy type but concealed a fair amount of sugar under its all too-solid flesh. Lunching with C C B Moss – a clever selector of clarets with independent ideas – one day, soon after I returned from service in 1919, I was shown the 1906 Ch La Lagune. I had never up till then fancied the vintage and, *pace* the '99 at the Wine Trade Club, had been apt to think slightingly of 'Lagune', but this wine – and it was the only occasion on which I have tasted it – seemed to me to be of outstanding merit, *bouqueté*, fruity and smooth and sweet. Both Haut-Brion and Cheval Blanc of 1906 were fine, sweet, beefy wines, though in their youth rather too coarse and heavy for frequent enjoyment. In addition to these two, the Brane-Cantenac also drinks well today. But on the whole, 1906s have displayed more beef than beauty. It was rash of me, however, to disparage Château La Lagune. I had an astonishing revelation of its keeping powers when I lunched with Hugh Rudd and Tony Berry (a son of Francis) at No three St James's Street, in January 1943. After giving us a bottle of '99 Lafite, followed by one of '68 Lafite, Major Hugh, always adventurous, produced a bottle of 1858 Ch La Lagune which was really quite notable and still very much alive in spite of its age. It never could have had the quality and rare distinction of the

Lafite and some others of the year I recollect to have met, but it was a born aristocrat. I see I mentioned it in my notebook as 'remarkable, jaded, but clean, and impression of sweet'. It deserved a more romantic epitaph as it was clearly a Lady of the Lake.

Another La Lagune that comes to my mind and ought to have modified my attitude was the 1907, a curiously flavoured but light, pretty wine of which that grand old all-round sportsman, Reading Grantham, wine-lover and merchant, who still lives in Sherborne at the ripe old age of ninety, had a few hogsheads. The Lagune struck his fancy as it had mine and he did not have to keep it very long in his cellars, but, like all 1907s, it was lacking in stamina and, though deliciously delicate and flavoury in youth, became plain and rather 'vacant' in its latter days, say in the early 'thirties. If a claret pleases and satisfies the critical eye, nose and palate on its twenty-first birthday, that is, when it comes of age, I think it may be said to have been a success, and the longer it pleases after that the more justifiable its claim to be so accounted. We are very apt in this country to assume that wine when young is not to be enjoyed. I have already pointed out that the 1875s were occupying a place of honour on the menus of Bordeaux society in 1884. They were then nine years old. Today, we almost excuse ourselves if we offer our friends a 1929 which, for the purpose of the generalization, might be comparable to 1875, and the '29s are already over fifteen years old. Development, it is true, will, in this climate, probably be more tardy than in Bordeaux, just as vintage ports bottled here come to maturity more slowly than those bottled at the same date in Oporto. Bordeaux and Oporto cellars are mostly overground whereas ours here are mostly underground: that would also account for a slower and perhaps really better development. But we neglect a good gamble in pleasure, I feel sure, by not starting to drink our wines, and particularly our clarets, a bit earlier than we usually do. I remember well William Hardie of Edinburgh giving me a bottle of Léoville 1888 after a day's fishing on Loch Leven, the magniloquent angler's paradise, in 1893, which was excellent: had he postponed drinking it for another two or three years it would, owing to the constitution of the vintage, have greatly deteriorated and given us little or no enjoyment. But then William Hardie knew how and when to discriminate.

I still hear from Grantham, though his letters are now written by another hand and he only signs them, but a very few years before the Second Great War burst upon us I received a letter from him asking me to go with him to a friend's house to dinner. He had been invited to bring someone with him who could appraise the virtues and value of old claret. So flattered was I at being considered by him to possess this qualification that I accepted. A beautiful house in a beautiful part of Dorset, a charming host, at some time I believe Lord-Lieutenant of the County, a most gracious hostess and a good dinner: what more could one ask for? Yes, quite right, and we got it, good wine. 1893 Ch Latour followed by 1875 Ch Latour – both were fine and the former on this occasion finer and more vigorous than the latter; but it seemed to me that both were palpably spoiled by having been slightly warmed, and, when asked my opinion of them, I said so, reluctantly but as plainly as good manners permitted. My host was horrified; such a thing could not happen in his house: my hostess was conciliatory and all for making allowances for me. My foster-host, Grantham, was, perhaps purposely, dumb, and, in view of my host's protestations, I myself was full of shame and apologies; and the incident passed over like a short-lived summer storm. After dinner we all sat before a comfortable fire between which and ourselves was an exquisite Buhl bean-shaped table and, on it, glasses sparkling in the firelight, a dish of fruit and a decanter of port. We had all resumed our normal demeanour and geniality and I had evidently been forgiven. 'Now, Grantham,' said our host, 'tell us what the port is', and except perhaps in the Factory House in Oporto, I rarely remember enjoying a glass of port under more ideal conditions. 'Well,' said Grantham, twisting his glass round and sipping again, 'it's a Cockburn.' 'Right,' said our host, 'what vintage?', and we all chortled and refilled to taste again. In my mind there were only two possible vintages, 1863 and 1868. That appears to have been in Grantham's mind, too, but, fortunately, the question had been put to him and not me. '1863' he hazarded, for one generally and out of courtesy hazards the older when in doubt. 'Wrong,' said our host, 'perhaps Colonel Campbell can tell us?' There was nothing else left for me to say, so out it came, '1868'. 'Well done, Cockburn's 1868 it is.' I claim no credit. Grantham gave the shipper and if I had been asked about the vintage first it is probable that I would have said 1863 and then Grantham pass me at the tape with 1868. But it really brought about some recovery of status to me and, less than a week later, further recovery followed when Grantham wrote me that he had just had a line from our host to say that his wretched parlourmaid had confessed to having washed the claret decanters in hot water just before the two Latours had been decanted into them. So, honesty had been the best policy after all: it is worth risking.

Horace Vachell once gave us a bottle of 1868 Cockburn at his Golden House at Bath, which was exquisite: he was proud of it and gratified at our appreciation. I wish I were capable of epitomizing the charms of his own Widcombe Manor: perhaps another time.

Eustace (Jerry) Oldham, too, who dabbled in old wine as well, and apparently as successfully, as he did in stocks and shares, gave us at his Ockham house on one occasion another very fine bottle of the Cockburn 1868. But the dinner of his I remember best was one at which we had four 1908 vintage ports to taste against each other. Preceding them was a magnum of 1920 Domaine de Chevalier, a wine of which I had acquired, when in Bordeaux, all the bottles and magnums I could lay hold of during one of my visits to the château: every Bordeaux vineyard likes to be called 'Château'. It was light, a little too discreet in the matter of bouquet, but soft, velvety and sweet and, as the Bordelais would say, *facile à boire*. André Simon often declared it to be the ideal of claret but, alas, it has had its day and is flickering out. The Saintsbury Club still possess some magnums on which I hope the cellarer will keep his weather eye. But to return to Jerry Oldham's delightful party – one of many – there were six men guests and Mrs Oldham and Jerry. From their infancy the 1908 ports, in my opinion, always possessed a charm of simplicity (*simplex munditiis,* Horace, who also loved his wine, called it) that is rarely found in other vintages: they were almost ready to drink on the day in 1910 that they were put into bottle. This might have foreshadowed a very early demise, and there are those who maintain that they and their attractive rivals, the 1912s, are both going rapidly downhill. Be that as it may, I am among those who still admire both vintages. Cockburn's and

Taylor's 1912 are for me splendid wines today, but I lean with unchanging fidelity to the, generally speaking, more spontaneously appealing and delicately flavoured 1908. The competition between the four champions of 1908 was very amusing and had been organized by our host with scrupulous and affectionate care. The decanters were numbered one to four and our glasses were numbered one to four, and no one but Jerry knew which shipper's wine each number represented. With one accord we all put out No three: it was difficult to say where the fault lay – it may have been in the bottle, as the wine was not as good as we all felt it ought to be. No. two was the next to go out; good appearance but very backward. This ena-dena-dina-dust method left Nos. one and four to fight it out, and by a majority of one the decision went to No one. Mrs Oldham, who had not assisted at the competition, curiously and cleverly enough confirmed the verdict when she was invited to taste and give her opinion. Graham and Taylor were the winners of this neck-to-neck, lip-to-lip, tongue-to-tongue contest. As the Graham man I was very gratified but must confess that I had given my vote to the Taylor!

Mais, revenons à nos moutons: I seem to have wandered a long way from my survey of claret vintages though 1907 claret is chronologically akin to 1908 port. Of 1908 clarets, as of the dead, let us say nothing, but of the 1909 a word or two since they were light and pleasing wines. My Bordeaux friends were surprised, I think, when I told them that I considered they would be popular in England: though an ultra-patriotic Scot, I am generally *Anglais* abroad, and anyway, in my opinion, 1909s were suitable for England but too light for the more rigorous northern climes. As I have said before, one of the first requisites I look for in claret is sugar, natural sugar after the must of the grapes has undergone a complete fermentation, and, quite recently, at Hugh Rudd's hospitable board in St James's Street, I have had several opportunites of discovering that '09s still retain a very good modicum of sweetness though the wines themselves are distinctly weary and wan. It is a pity good things have to die as surely as bad things, but kindness seems ever to live. When enemy action knocked my business and myself off our balance, and very nearly out of the ring altogether, Rudd, with generous impulse, invited me to lunch one Tuesday, which we called *Mardi Gras*, and then bade me come every Tuesday. That was in May 1941, and now, in September 1945, the pleasurable habit of *Mardi Gras* still persists!

In spite of Maurice Healy's pronounced admiration of the 1910 Haut-Brion – so near akin, he would have it, to O'Brien – I must refuse to say a word in favour of the vintage. Oh, yes, I tasted the Haut-Brion, at Maurice's own invitation, but I fear it must have been when it was past its best as the lure of Hibernian incantations and songs of praise were of no effect. I remained unrepentant and obstinate in my view that it was a thin, acetic, mildewed mockery of a claret, with a meretricious bouquet which could not conceal its defects. Scent also has that failing. Maurice's predilection for Haut-Brion was common knowledge but he went too far again when he claimed that the 1906 Haut-Brion was the finest claret of a generation. It is very good, but …! On the other hand I have had one or two fairly nice 1911 clarets in Denmark Street, Bristol, and elsewhere, but I cannot remember tasting one that was, or is, really outstanding: the same applies to many passingly good vintages which are not only welcome in themselves but are also useful foils to lead up to the highlights.

The 1912 vintage produced many attractive wines but they were mostly the victims of mildew and have never become either reliable or popular; nor have I ever seen a 1913 that had not a fatal resemblance to 1910. There was what the French call a '*manque d'agrément*' in both vintages. We have all had our disappointments in clarets: if we had not, all the Bordeaux shippers would be millionaires and all their agents treated like Delphic oracles. 1912 was disappointing but 1914 was even more so. When they were still young, in 1920, they were full of promise and seemed to B E F fellows coming back from France, with its arbitrary choice of '*vinn rooge*' or '*vinn blank*', quite the best thing in claret they had seen for years and years. I bought a few bottles of the Margaux from one of my old friends and put them in my cellar. Suddenly a collapse came. As lovely dahlias in full bloom will be smitten by the first frost of autumn, and die where they stand, so the 1914s, Margaux included, alas! suddenly faded away and died as it were in a night. Dead rustling leaves that collect in the gutter and through which children love to strut (at least I did seventy years ago) best describe the smell they took on, and both their colour and their flavour were similarly withered and dun: a keen disappointment.

The 1915s were of the same calibre as the '13s and '10s and of the same acidulated complexion. I never saw a good one, but 1916, too hard, 1917, too unstable, 1918, too leathery, all showed an occasional good and even attractive wine, chiefly in the medium qualities, though their vintages, as a whole, were uneven and unsatisfactory, and forced into consumption far too young and at far too high a price owing to the unleashed demand after the First World War. One of my partners once said during this period that he wished he had a dictaphone to record my changeable views on some of the '16s and '17s! The combination of green, hard immaturity and exorbitant prices will never do any good to the cult of Bordeaux which, say what we will about the artistic appeal and charm of claret, always requires careful guidance and nursing. The taste for claret is still, as far as this country is concerned, an acquired one, too delicate to be wantonly undermined.

The 1919s as far as I am concerned may join the 1915s, 1913s and 1910s, though I have heard people say they were 'quite nice', which is as damning as calling Mrs So-and-So a 'worthy woman'.

CHAPTER 6

Clarets of the Early 'Twenties

Independence of Taste. C B C as an Amateur. '20 and '23. Léoville and Larose. '23 Cheval Blanc. Sequence of Service. What about '24? Omar Khayyám Club.

We come now to a decade of vintages of more immediate and practical interest, and if I express an opinion on them I am more open to criticism and correction than when throwing my weight about in connection with the older vintages. It may have been noticed that, in passing judgement on vintages, I have refrained from specifying more than one or two of the first, or second, or more prominent 'growths' of a year. More often than not it is by these that the fame, the success or failure, of a vintage is assessed, and I fear it would become very tedious for any reader to have to wade through long lists of wines accompanied by my individual opinion on each. I have protested elsewhere that this is not intended to be a textbook or a catalogue, but I hope that, nevertheless, it may give an inquiring student a sufficient idea of the characteristics to look for in some wines and successive vintages to enable him to speak intelligently with his wine merchant who, I am sure, will always be glad to add that gratifying practical experience, an ounce of which is so much more valuable than tons of book-knowledge. Wine, like all expressions of art, must be a matter of personal and individual taste, and everybody, whether amateur or professional, may assert his own preferences; and who is to say he is right or wrong save those who agree or disagree with him? I always try to encourage those companions tasting wine with me, to say out exactly what they think, if they think anything at all. When you have good amateurs with you it is a pleasurable observance to give them something fine. C B Cochran, for example, kind courteous gentleman in good days and bad, is one who, apt to be shy in pushing his opinion, is ready to give it with knowledge and conviction: I would back his verdict against that of many a professional. He, too, is a Saintsburian, and was a member in old days of several jolly parties at the Hind's Head and the retailer of many a good story of his own experiences. Are they not written in the book of *Cock-a-Doodle-do* and others of his reminiscences?

There must be many and various verdicts upon the 1920 vintage clarets. They were well constituted wines with good colour and bouquet and flavour, but to my taste most of them, and some people will say all of them, were disappointingly dry. That is where I always maintain that clarets of recent years, however fine they are, fail when compared with the older vintages, and I ask myself if this is due to modern methods of vinification or to a global change in climatic conditions, or what? The 1920s were, and are, dry and yet many of them are so good to drink that it seems ungracious to be too critical about their shortcomings. The Léoville-Poyferré, pre-eminently, and one or two other second 'growths' are welcome guests on any table, and the Haut-Brion, the Cheval Blanc, the Chevalier, the Latour, particularly the last named, show unquestionably very

fine qualities and sometimes leave an impression of real sweetness. It is curious how variable they all are but that is typical of
modern tendency. I may have more to say about the Latour at a
future date; it appeared at the classic banquets of the Vintners'
Company for several years and won the approbation of King
Edward VIII when he was Prince of Wales: but, as Kipling
would say, that is another story and to me a not uninteresting
one. Between those of 1900 and 1928 the 1920 vintage stands
out as the all-round best.

There was one gorgeously outstanding 1921, the Ch Cheval
Blanc, a truly magnificent claret and, like an exception proving
a rule, full of sugar, too full perhaps to escape the attention of
the germ of aceticism which I fear is always lurking round the
corner, for even its sugar must conform to the equal balance of
a wine. There were other drinkable 1921s but none to rival the
incomparable Cheval Blanc about which I have already spoken
at some length.

The 1922 was not shipped generally to this country, but I
have drunk some of its wines in France. They are soft and gentle
and possess no marked personality and little attraction.

On the contrary 1923 is, or, should I say, has been, a very
intriguing and fascinating vintage. I think I must have been
among the first to introduce its wines into this country because
I remember being taunted by some of my competitors on their
'watery' appearance. But, acknowledging that they were very
light as *débutants* and probably lacking in stamina, I found,
when I first saw them in Bordeaux, an agreeable and unusual
bouquet and that yearning-to-be-sweet farewell that had drawn
me to 1905 and 1909. I called them 'Wine Merchants' Wines',
here today and gone tomorrow and very pleasant while they

last. Some merchants would not touch them, others more venturesome and discerning, bought freely and, I think, have been glad they did so. I never pretended they would make old bones but, at 3 St. James's Street in the summer of this year (1945), I enjoyed with Hugh Rudd and others a bottle of the Haut-Brion which was extremely winsome and still as sound as a bell. My doctor, Edward F Griffith, to whom I introduced the Haut-Brion, maintains that it is the most perfect claret he has ever drunk. He is probably not far wrong as his experience has been confined to ordinary and consequently less impressive wines, but he has a good conscientious palate and will never go back to 'Ordinaire' at two and sixpence a bottle or even 'Très Ordinaire' at three and six!

Since the 1923 I have not seen a Ch Haut-Brion that I considered worthy of the old champion's worldwide reputation, but I am hopeful of the 1937 which seemed to me, just before the War began, with others of the same vintage, to show promise of better things. A particularly attractive '23 was the Ch Larose-Faure. Unfortunately, in my opinion, the vineyard of Larose-Faure (or Larose-Bethmann as it is sometimes, and as correctly, called) has been reunited with that of the Larose-Sarget which, again in my own opinion, was less successfully cultivated for many years; true, it had had intermittently a marked success in some of the older years, such as 1905 and others not particularly celebrated, and in 1920 it was distinctly good. The same fate I am told possibly awaits the Léoville-Poyferré, which presumably would be re-amalgamated with the Léoville-Lascases which of late years has been generally much inferior to the Poyferré section of this famous vineyard, though under the same caretaker and cultivator. Indeed, I think most claret lovers esteem Poyferré of recent years as very closely approaching the excellence of a first growth. In 1923 it was charming and more full to the taste than the majority of the Médoc wines of that year, but not than the Lafite and Latour, which, for some reason or another, were much darker in colour, and bigger and fatter than their contemporaries. I have heard Léoville and Larose called sister wines: they are definitely feminine and with pretty names that one cannot but associate with pretty wines. May they always be so. A curious fact, or illusion, I might mention here was that a 1920 vintage wine never showed well after a 1923, although in popular as well as expert estimation much finer. There must have been some invisible but constitutional antagonism. *Apropos* of Léoville, an old friend of mine, who was once invited to stand as Conservative candidate for Chelsea and turn Sir Charles Dilke out, asked me to dine with him, when I was a young man, and gave me a glass of 1874 Ch Léoville out of a bottle which he had opened four days previously for a guest and kept for me because he knew I had a liking and taste for fine claret! He was an elderly gentleman and I was young and had been brought up to be polite, so I drank the claret and thanked him for his 'kind thought'. Please note that claret of all wines should be drunk up at the meal for which it has been uncorked. No, I have not forgotten that '58 Lafite; a grand exception on that occasion.

I have already mentioned the 1923 Ch Cheval Blanc with its sweet sunny flavour and somewhat exotic redolence and great charm. It was light, very light, but possessed of a refined firmness and individuality. The Cheval Blanc would, if necessary, have made a reputation for the '23s just as it did for the '21s. I remember that at one dinner of the Saintsbury Club the '23 Cheval Blanc was served. I happened to be occupying the chair on that occasion and that gifted fellow Scot, Colonel Walter Elliot, no mean judge of wine, was on my right, with a vacant chair next to him for his parliamentary colleague, Lord Lymington (now Earl of Portsmouth), who arrived late. Elliot had kept him a glass of the claret and, when he arrived, told him he had done so and, without saying what the wine was, asked him what he thought of it. Lymington looked at it critically, smelt it carefully and sipped it. 'I call that a little racehorse,' said he. 'You are right,' said Elliot, 'it's the 1923 Ch Cheval Blanc.' The incident gave me great pleasure. As a matter of fact I have found that most Members of Parliament, whatsoever their political views may be, enjoy their glass of wine and are appreciative of quality: some are genuine amateurs.

There is much virtue in the sequence in which wine vintages are served. Normally, one should serve the youngest wine first and the oldest last. The real connoisseur, the old hand, will lead up to his showpiece and, from time to time, may serve a younger wine after an older. It is unusual, but I have seen an individual 1875 served successfully after an 1874, for instance, and a 1900 after an 1899. Rendlesham, at one of his lunches, interposed two 1864s, the Léoville and the Lafite, between 1875 Branaire and a magnum of 1874 Haut-Brion which was a celebrated giant of its day and stood well up to the test; but other friends of mine tried 1878 after 1870 and failed to satisfy either themselves or their guests. I would not like to discourage experiments which illustrate a search for knowledge on the part of the zealous amateur. My friend Israel Sieff is one of these and has enunciated a theory that the proper order of serving claret should be not by sequence of age or selection of vintage, but by weight of wine from the lightest wine at the start to the stoutest wine for a finish. When I dined with him, for instance, one evening, my menu of which unfortunately was destroyed in the blitz – and the vintages I mention are all hypothetical – we began with, perhaps, a 1923 and went on to an 1875, then back to 1899 and on to 1870, finishing up with 1921 Cheval Blanc. I am afraid my sequence may be incorrect but we certainly finished up with the '21 after much older wines. It was an exhilarating adventure, and all the wines were tip top of their respective years, but I went away unconvinced that my friend's theory, though an undoubted tribute to imagination and initiative, could ever be put into general practice with æsthetic approbation. I still favour chronological sequence in the serving of clarets, that is from youth to age, unless expert knowledge demands some modification. Quite recently, for example, in the summer of 1945, Hugh Rudd gave me an ideal sequence of clarets which I think would also have satisfied Sieff's ideology. The wines were 1923 Ch Haut-Brion, 1900 Ch Léoville-Poyferré, 1875 Ch Palmer and 1870 Ch Lafite, in that order, each wine showing exemplary condition and fitness, even the Palmer, which is one of the few '75s, surely, that has preserved something of its youthful freshness, sweetness, and the typical sunny flavour of its year.

A similar service in sequence would, by and large, apply to port, burgundy, hock, moselle and champagne and any other wines designated by their vintage years. It might not apply to brandy, whose declared vintage, for many years, certainly prior to fifty years ago, was too often but the echo of historical romance or the spiritualistic reincarnation of mythical sagas.

Whether 1923s will live much longer, and whether the

bleak weariness of senescence has or has not already over-shadowed some, many, of them I would not like to say. Last autumn, Douglas West, amateur of wine, 'borrowed' Corney & Barrow's comfortable luncheon igloo, carved out of their spacious arched cellars, and gave us a jeroboam of the 1923 Ch Larose-Faure which was fine, firm and fruity: first rate, with no signs of decay. One guest likened it to 'bottled sulphur'; he meant it as a compliment but it sounded somewhat left-handed: nevertheless, I have noticed at times that the '64 Lafite, when first uncorked, exhaled an unmistakable whiff of sulphur. In any case, the 1923s have served a good purpose for twenty years and to some extent made up for the unexpected disap-pointment of 1924s. It is not that these latter are bad wines: on the contrary they seemed to be constitutionally very healthy and well made, somewhat in the image of and of the same size and build as the 1920s, and at the outset rather sweeter. But like a boy who shows signs of promise and then fails in his examinations for the profession he was going to adorn, so the 1924s have, up to now, failed to stand the test, simply from a kind of indolence and inability to display the good quality that is undoubtedly there. Very disappointing. I use the expres-sion 'up to now' because I am still hoping that some of them, and particularly the Pauillac triumvirate, Lafite, Latour and Mouton, may eventually redeem the reputation of the vintage and justify our early expectation. One day they please and one's hopes revive, only to be dashed on the morrow. Barry Neame, at the Hind's Head Hotel at Bray, was famous for his wine parties, and I recollect that he had a series of three or four din-ners of six (the perfect number for a small intimate party) to compare the respective merits of 1920, 1923 and 1924. At one dinner we would have, say, the Cheval Blanc and Ausone of the three years, at another the Lafite and Latour, and so on, i.e. six bottles of wine each time for the six jurymen who were all claret drinkers and most of them connected with the wine trade. A consensus of opinion gave 1920 an easy first on points; 1923 and 1924 were close together with the balance, if I remember rightly, in favour of 1923 by a small margin. Barry – 'Mine Host' – as he called himself, was *sui generis* a great innkeeper and outstanding showman, bluff, jovial, outspoken (sometimes yclept 'rude') and warmhearted, and I met many interesting people and gathered much useful information at the then, and still, under the capable managership of Miss Williams, hospitable Hind's Head at Bray.[1]

I think 1924 clarets needed, and still need, very careful decanting and serving. Well served, as at a Vintners' banquet, they please, anyhow up to a point, but carelessly served as they were at a certain restaurant, where I dined with the Omar Khayyám Club some years ago, they tasted crude and disconcerting. It is good that there should be an Omar Khayyám Club as well as a Saintsbury Club, and one day perhaps we shall have an André Simon Club. I went to dine with the Omar as guest of the late Professor Henry Armstrong, who was one of the biggest chemists of his day but had to sit under the chairmanship of a particle of a corpuscle like myself as a member of the Board of Governors of St Dunstan's College, Catford. He did not seem to bear me any ill-will on that account. He was too big. I received a white carnation for my buttonhole on arrival, and, in proposing the toast of the guests, Sir Herbert Samuel

---

[1] Poor Barry died not very long after these words were written.

84

(now Lord Samuel) pointed out that all the guests had been given white carnations, 'emblems of your blameless lives', he said, adapting Tennyson, and adding 'we members, you will note, wear scarlet carnations'.

There was some inconsequential controversy about 1925s, but, in my opinion, they failed in all essential respects. Thin and watery, without balance and with insufficient sugar to create it. One advocate, Francis Leslie, well known for what Horace Vachell would call his 'expertise' in port wine, made me the present of a dozen bottles of the Château Margaux, to convince me of the error of my ways, but they ganged agley. I had an excellent opportunity, too, of giving the vintage a fair trial in the snug little hotel at Sligachan in the Isle of Skye. It nestles on the loch side at the foot of the majestic and mysterious massif known as the Cuillins, where the kelpies and the 'little people' hold sway. On a wine-list remarkable in so remote a spot I found the Lafite, Latour and Mouton, all of 1925. I sampled the three in turn and in conditions most favourable to them and they were all very second-rate, unresponsive and unsatisfying: poor tackle after a sunny day amid those immortal and most beautiful mountains.

CHAPTER 7

Later Vintages and Afterthoughts

More Beef Wanted? 1928 and 1929 Clarets. A M P Hodsoll. Robert Gibbings. Food with Wine. Cork-drawing. Temperature. '31 Haut-Brion-Blanc. War, its Vintages and Spurious Juices. Duties and Chancellors. Churchill. Horne. The Three Chamberlains. Bordeaux Visions.

The 1926s are, in my opinion, even though I have previously characterized them as somewhat hard and coarse, good wines, much neglected in youth owing to their expensiveness. They have plenty of sugar, and those of us of the old gang who survive should still get a good deal of enjoyment out of those that are left of them. We have a bigger choice nowadays than our fathers had before us because we do not confine our attentions only to the wines of the Médoc. The more fleshy and fruity wines of St Emilion and Pomerol, especially in years like 1926, have made (as have also, be it acknowledged, the beverage or 'dry' wines as they call them, of Australia and South Africa) great strides in popular favour during the last twenty or thirty years, possibly to satisfy a growing need, in these days of hustle and nerve strain, for the very qualities of fleshiness and fruitiness which charac-terize them. If only our Dominion friends would concentrate their efforts on the production of a Lafite or Yquem, a Romanée Conti or a white Musigny (such as that gem of 1919 vintage that

C M Wells gave the committee of the Saintsbury Club when he had them to lunch) instead of building on the shallow or, shall we say, shortsighted principle of mass production! That, however, is for another day, and the companionship I have been privileged to enjoy of protagonists like Cuthbert Burgoyne and Harry Bull has satisfied me that the *beau idéal* is not being overlooked.

But I digress. What a bad habit of mine it is! When we come to 1927 one recalls an old tag that went 'Oh, no, we never speak of her'. One rarely hears them mentioned, and there cannot be many of them in this country: although I discerned signs of disintegration, I have been surprised by the passableness of those I have drunk, so let us put them on a par with '25 and '19, and turn to the unquestionably more interesting competition evoked by the differing, but splendid, qualities of vintages 1928 and 1929. It brings one back to the rivalry between those still more famous vintages 1899 and 1900. Those of us who had the advantage of visiting Bordeaux, and driving through its ramification of vineyards in Médoc and the Graves and St Emilion, in or about 1930, will perhaps remember our first impressions of 1928 and 1929 and also the comments of the owners, *régisseurs* and *maîtres de chai*, who, one and all, seemed to have '99 and 1900 in their minds. I remember that my tastings and observations at the time led me at once to favour 1928. They seemed so well-balanced and well-bred, full to the taste and, at the same time, supple, which describes a characteristic that one must always look for in young wine, as in young human beings – something capable of responding to a call for better efforts to come. There was a touch of tannin and roughness about them, it is true, but it seemed to me to be counterbalanced by a sufficiency of fruit and sugar. I thought to myself 'these are fine wines with a sure future'. Their development, let me confess at once, has been much slower than I expected, and I must have misjudged the amount of tannin in them; but they are making good progress, if at a somewhat leisurely pace, and I still anticipate a noteworthy future for them, or for those that are left when restrictions on the importation of younger, and perhaps more 'ready', wines, have been removed. The latest bottle of the vintage I have shared, and it was quite recently, was one of the Ch Ausone, and I must say I found it first-rate and full of promise of a great future. It is interesting, too, to look back to the first bottle of a classed growth of 1928 that I drank, and it was with my wife at the sunny sea-girt hotel at Lochboisdale, on the island of South Uist, in the late summer of, I think, 1935. Finlay Mackenzie, the proprietor, mentioned to me that he had bought a few dozens of the Ch Margaux and would like me to pass judgement. I am afraid I disappointed him when I suggested that it should be kept for many years before being put on his wine-list, a suggestion which war stringency has probably prevented him from adopting. The wine was full-bodied but tasted cold and cheerless and showed little of the quality that I knew was there. Fortunately, the wine-list was an ample one, and the hotel generally so comfortable and efficient that I mentioned it to the Wine and Food Society for their special list. What a delightful house-party we were too! What fun the fishing that had drawn us all to the island! One of the fishermen, the most successful, if I remember rightly, was Sir Philip Christison, the brilliant general of today, who has so distinguished himself in the Burma campaign.

Praise of one vintage does not imply lack of esteem for others.

'I love not man the less but Nature more',

said Byron. Antony went so far as to declare that he loved and honoured both Cæsar and Brutus, and we can more easily, and more truly, love two rival consecutive vintages of claret. Let me go back to my first impressions of the 1929s. I found in them a small taste of over-ripe grapes: I do not like to use the word 'rotten' in case it sound condemnatory, and the imperfection hardly reached that stage: the wines seemed otherwise soft, mellow and very sweet, sweeter than the '28s whose sugar content was at any rate less obvious. It was not unnatural that one should feel a little nervous about their development. Would they keep long enough to be enjoyable to drink? The answer to that query is that as a vintage they have already done so, in spite of the fact that a few of them have already begun to show signs of distress and are getting edgy and losing that fragrance and sweetness that were their chief charm. If any of them win through and come safely to full maturity they should be superb, but I fear it may be, perhaps, a big 'if'. Let us drink them and enjoy them while the going is good and leave their future to take care of itself. *Apropos*, it may be interesting to note that Féret, in '*Bordeaux et ses Vins*', 1886 issue, encourages one to surmise that the 1834 vintage must rather have resembled the 1929 with a '*goût de pourriture assez prononcé*' in its early days: he states that this defect ultimately disappeared and the vintage became one of the most celebrated of the century! It might be worth while to risk binning away a few dozens of some of the '29s, among them Latour, Margaux and Mouton Rothschild – I do not so much fancy, perhaps, the Lafite, of which a friend of mine has laid down 100 dozens, and still less the Haut-Brion (*pace* Victor Bulley) – and sample a bottle of each annually on one of the many fine days usual in May or June, with a nice little saddle of lamb, or mutton, a Camembert cheese and a couple of friends (present company not necessarily excepted), and when it is considered that any of them has reached its zenith, or perfect maturity, to set to and drink the rest of the bin, alone, if you wish, but preferably with a few kindred spirits around your table. The quintessence of the enjoyment of good wine is the sharing of it with others. A M P Hodsoll, for some time my very valued deputy-chairman of the Wine and Spirit Association, gave A B Knowles and me a bottle of the '29 Mouton Rothschild at Claridge's, in the early autumn of 1945, which really touched the ideal of fine claret. Hodsoll's untimely death, after an operation, came as a terrible shock to his many friends, including myself. He seemed in his normal health, never robust but otherwise good, when the trouble developed. His cheeriness, his unselfishness and his kindness of nature endeared him to us all and I have ample reason to be grateful for his friendship. He loved his garden, he loved his books and, I think one may add, he loved his friends. Soon after it was published, I introduced him to Robert Gibbings' colourful book, *Lovely is the Lee*, as he found always a strong appeal in Irish humour; and how he enjoyed Robert's story of the bus drive from Inchigeela to Ballingeary and the befuddled old fellow-traveller who sang without intermission, except to implore Robert to join in:

'Red is the rose that in yonder garden grows
And fair is the lily of the vall–ey.'

Both Hodsoll and I were tickled by Robert's comment on 'the last syllable of "valley" jumping up into a high note from which there was no recovery'; and his concisely picturesque language is often on a par with the brilliant woodcuts with which he himself illustrates his books. I was present when Barry Neame brought Maurice Healy and Robert Gibbings together at one of his dinner parties and placed them next to each other at the table, two very portly Irishmen out of entirely different moulds, one dark, unhealthily pallid and cleanshorn and the other fair and profusely hirsute, but both of them gloriously gifted with an unlimited capacity for friendship and a quick natural wit that may be Hibernian but is intensely human. I need hardly add that Robert also, like all rational Irishmen, quizzes and enjoys his glass of wine and is very catholic in his choice, but not so articulate in broadcasting his opinion as was Maurice, whose sobriquet, as a member of Ye Odde Volumes, was 'The Prattler' which, being interpreted, means the man who can talk.

I must stress an important maxim in entertaining, which the reference above to lamb and mutton brings to mind, and that is the desirability of harmonizing what you eat with what you drink, or vice versa. Many a bottle of fine delicately matured wine has been rendered nugatory, tasteless and wasteful by being served along with some strong and highly flavoured culinary masterpiece. As André Simon says, for instance, the only beverage to drink with curry is water, or, he might have added, beer, but not wine. Many fish dishes, delightful in themselves, will preclude the enjoyment of red wine and should preferably be accompanied by white, and so on. The Wine and Food Society will give full advice to seekers after knowledge. I mention this simply because so many ambitious hosts and hostesses select the sequence of the food with unremitting care, such-and-such an entrée leading up to such-and-such a joint, and a particular savoury following well after a particular sweet, and so on, but they never think about the tuning-in of the wines: consequently they remain an ambitious host and hostess without ever becoming good ones. It is a mistake, however, to err in the other direction and become too fussy: fastidious impeccability in the complementary selection of food and drink is demanded when entertaining; for the solitary individual, or in the family circle, such would be profligate, even if not practically impossible. When I was young it was almost a sin to enjoy one's food, let alone one's liquor. If we are in the habit of drinking a bottle of claret, or white wine, or beer, with our dinner it would be absurd and extravagant to insist upon the provision always of selected and suitable food. The lot of the poor lady of the house, the materfamilias, would be a purgatory. The Council of the Wine and Food Society will, I hope, accord me dispensation for a pronouncement so dietetically unorthodox but, in my opinion, so safeguarded by common sense and the ethics of domestic economy. There are certain duties to all your wines that can be paid without much extra trouble. The corkscrew can be pointed straight down the centre of the cork for instance, not askew, and driven in to the full length of the cork to prevent it breaking up. And another tip which takes less than no trouble is to avoid serving your claret warmed or 'with the chill off', as it is euphemistically called. All artificial heating, either of the wine or the decanter, endangers, and sometimes kills, the life of the wine. Wine, even after years in bottle, is still a living entity and susceptible to good or ill treatment.

During the First World War, a very dear brother officer of mine in the Argyll and Sutherland Highlanders invited me to dine with him in one of the hotels in Dunoon and, knowing, as he said, and as my old Chelsea friend had said, that I enjoyed a glass of good claret, he had had a bottle of the 1899 Ch Lafite decanted and put before the fire 'to take the chill off.' How long it had occupied the cosy grate I do not know, but when it came to the table columns of smoke were streaming out of it. The wine was almost at the boil, and my good comrade and kinsman suggested that perhaps 'they' had warmed it too much! In my opinion it is safer and better to serve the wine quite cold, and warm it with the heat of your hand round the glass, than to give orders to the waiter to 'take the chill off'. Even at the old Wellington Club, when I lunched or dined there, I used to give strict injunctions that neither my claret, nor the decanter into which it was going, nor my wine-glass were to be warmed; and, even then, sometimes, I failed to out-manœuvre the ingrained cussedness and deadly habit of some wine-butler. The ideal temperature for claret is the temperature of the room in which it is to be drunk.

Of the vintages 1930, 1931 and 1932 the less said, perhaps, the better, but I shall look forward to the day when some devotee of one or other of them will produce a really fine bottle of any. The 1931, white wine, of the Ch Haut-Brion, however, was excellent. Many of us were ignorant of the fact that the proprietors of the famous old vineyard had surrounded it with a belt of white grape vines until we were introduced to this 1931, but, if they can produce so good and attractive a white wine in an 'off' year like 1931, may they go on and prosper. It is relatively far superior to the red wine of the same year and growth which the Wine and Food Society gave us at one of their periodical banquets.

The 1933 is light, sound and pleasant: 'very good luncheon wine' I have often described it, and I have a sentimental *penchant* for the Ch Beychevelle, of which the entire crop was purchased by my generous St. James's Street friends, who know well my unabashed and perpetual admiration of it. I have had occasion more than once to compare it with the Beychevelle 1934 which, belonging to a better vintage, is probably a better wine, but the '33 holds its own marvellously well even in such good company. I think that some of the 1933s, such as the Mouton Rothschild and others, will turn up trumps and surprise those who are apt to decry their many good but, perhaps, rather un-emphasized features. 1934, as I have already said, is, in my opinion, a better vintage, and I shall not be astonished if one day it comes to be looked upon as outstanding. Since our habitual deliberateness leads us to consider it too young to exploit today there may be a fair quantity of the vintage left for our future delectation. With the memory of past disappointments always in mind it may be unwise to prophesy, but 1934s have a balance of body, bouquet and sugar in them to justify great expectations. There may be, but I have not yet met any, poor or bad wines amongst them, as there invariably are in the best of vintages, just as in the reverse sense there is scarcely a vintage, however ill-esteemed and miserable, that cannot show one or two plums: the difficulty is to spot and secure them early enough!

Since 1934 we have had the 1935, admittedly poor on all counts, the 1936, sound, clean wines but without, in my opinion, allure; and the 1937, stout and rather dry, but possessing a certain suppleness and agreeable flavour, the kind of vintage in which, again in my own opinion, the *bourgeois* and *artisan* wines will have a better wicket to bat on than the classed growths: that, too, remains to be seen, and indeed all my comments and expressions of opinion on the last twenty-five years' vintages are open to contradiction by those whose experiences have been, and will be, different from mine. It is an exciting prospect. 1938, light, sweetish and attractive, will be useful and perhaps something better: *nous verrons*.

Through the kindness of Hugh Rudd I have seen one or two samples of each of the War years, and of these, after their hazardous journey, the representatives of 1942 and 1943 appeared to be the most promising, and the 1944 the lightest, but sweetest. Such information as I have so far been able to gather direct from Bordeaux indicates that 1940 and 1943, and probably not 1942, are the best of the War years. Since news emanating from Reims and the Côte d'Or also favours 1943 as being of exceptionally fine quality it seems quite possible that that year may become celebrated among wine lovers.

I have already admitted that I have mentioned in the course of my sketchy survey of claret only the *premiers crus*, or higher growths, of the different vintages, but it has been due to the general success, or failure, of most of its better-classed wines that a vintage has or has not become famous. One swallow (I allude to the bird) will not make a summer, and one or two successes in a bad year will rarely do much to enhance the final verdict on that year, nor one or two failures damn a good vintage. The excellence of the 1880 Mouton Rothschild did not avert the condemnation of its vintage, nor did the quite remarkably fine quality of 1921 Cheval Blanc constitute the vintage of that otherwise poor year a success. The sorry fate of 1928 Ch Lafite and poor showing of 1929 Ch Haut-Brion did nothing to detract from the fame of these two vintages and on the other hand, the admirable quality of many of the less-known Médoc and St. Emilion wines of 1916 and 1917 did not succeed in making these vintages popular or renowned. It is the Churchills and Roosevelts and Stalins that make a generation historically famous and not you or I, dear reader, whatever merits (or demerits) we may inwardly know we possess.

When one remembers the hidden wealth of sugar in the stubborn 1870s, and the neglected but exquisite beauty of the delicate 1871s that followed them, one can only hope that *les années de la guerre* may again prove the hand of untrammelled Nature to be a not unsuccessful substitute for the skilled labour of Man. If 1944 only proved to be another 1871, none of us, perhaps, would mind paying the some ten times higher price that Bordeaux shippers are already, and without guarantee of any sort, asking for it today! What with the exorbitant and short-sighted demands of my friends, the Bordeaux shippers, and the restrictive, almost prohibitive, duty on claret and light wines generally imposed by our own equally short-sighted legislators, it looks as though Gladstone's meritorious effort to encourage the consumption of low-strength beverage wines is destined to the scrap heap; and that, wine being henceforth an expensive luxury, against Gladstone's advice, our middle classes, if they cannot for one reason or another drink beer or spirits, will take, for their alcoholic refreshment, one or other of those fermented fruit juices (by no means always grape juice) which are dangled before an easily gulled public and to which I have already drawn attention. Beware of them. Providence has ordained that Britain shall not be by nature a wine-producing country; this should be borne in mind by those, of whom there seems to be an increasing number, who possess œnophilous ambitions and wish to indulge in the, at present, tantalizing pastime of a search for wine, genuine wine. It is they who should insist on a lowering of duties. The wine trade itself might appear to be too much of an interested party, even though its demands are largely on behalf of the purchasing public. I have been on several deputations to sundry Chancellors of the Exchequer to discuss policy and protest against the ever-increasing burden of duties. One of the most memorable, in view of the capricious circumstances of the present day, was a visit to Mr Winston Churchill when he was Chancellor. With his most winning smile and a cigar in the corner of his mouth he told us that he wanted more money out of us, and we had to point out the growing danger to the wine trade of 'British Wine', which at that time was paying an unjustifiably small excise duty as 'British Sweets!' Churchill, with a twinkle in his eye, said, 'I must remind you, gentlemen, that Great Britain is still a part of the British Empire and entitled to some preference'! In the friendly atmosphere the Chancellor engendered I asked him, 'What did Mr Gladstone do in 1860–61?' He turned to me, took the cigar out of his mouth and replied with most engaging simplicity: 'Ah! you must remember that Mr Gladstone was a very great man dealing with comparatively small figures, whereas I am a small man dealing with gigantic figures'. Not the answer that, at that time, one would have expected from Winston Churchill. We know him better now; we have discovered the inspiration of his leadership and the grandeur of his humility. I told this story of his father to Major Randolph Churchill when I met him at lunch at Chalié Richards' office, and he had it published in the 'Londoner's Diary' of the *Evening Standard*. I enjoyed, too, a rather more intimate conversation with the late Robert Horne (subsequently Lord Horne) when he was Chancellor of the Exchequer. He refused to receive a deputation but eventually agreed to see me alone. I happened to be playing my first innings as chairman of the Wine and Spirit Association that year. We chatted for a good hour, and I heard every reason under the sun why a reduction in duties was an economic and national impossibility, and, when we had exhausted the topic and touched on others, he turned to me and said with a chuckle, 'As one Scot to another, Campbell, tell me where the devil I can buy some good brandy at a reasonable price'.

Neville Chamberlain was somewhat sinister and forbidding to look at but very human and very logical when it came to talking: I was on deputations to him more than once, and he gave the impression of being straight and understanding; his refusals were always gently, and almost deferentially, given; a very charming character. Austen Chamberlain, when we met him, appeared cold and nervous, and changed his monocle for pince-nez, and pince-nez for horn-rimmed spectacles, and spectacles back to pince-nez or monocle the whole time he was talking, but he was strong and forthright in speech and pulled up very severely one speaker, who was foolishly exaggerating part of our case, our deplorable impoverishment and our hidden power; shaking his forefinger at him, and changing his monocle for his spectacles (or vice versa, I cannot remember), Chamberlain replied, 'I have all your income tax returns before me, refuting your arguments, and shall know how to deal with you if you attempt to take any of the steps you threaten'. That speaker, I need hardly say, had shot his bolt and I do not know what became of him.

I came, posthumously, so to speak, into contact also with Joseph Chamberlain, the still more distinguished father of these two distinguished statesmen. His widow, who became, by her remarriage, Mrs Carnegie, very generously contributed to one of the Red Cross Wine Sales held during the recent War three bottles of Chartreuse which Mr Chamberlain had taken into his cellar in 1895 and on which the dust of ages lay so thick that, as Mrs Carnegie wrote, she was not sure whether the liqueur was 'green' or 'yellow'. When, as chairman of the organizing committee, I wrote to thank her, she took the trouble to reply and say, 'It gives me much satisfaction to feel how appropriate it is that I have been able to send a small contribution which is associated with the name of Mr Chamberlain, for there is no cause which he would have had more at heart than the splendid work which is being done for our prisoners of war and other purposes by the Red Cross'. Tom Restell, the ever-cheery auctioneer, through the agency of whose inspiring hammer the painfully struggling Wine and Spirit Trade contributed over £140,000 to the coffers of the Red Cross and St John Fund, told me that it was the great age and loss of colour of the liqueur inside the bottles, and not the dust on their outside, that made it impossible to announce for certain whether the Chartreuse was green or yellow. The three bottles fetched £62 and found a home, I hope, worthy of their history.

I make no excuse for having concentrated the story of my experiences so much on claret, the most natural and fascinating of wines, of infinite variety and unfailing interest, an easy and informative teacher, the mother of the family of wine. I would that I had the pen and mellow terminology of some of my old friends like Stephen Gwynn, Warner Allen or André Simon, to make the story more graphic, seductive and helpful.

'I would that my tongue could utter
The thoughts that arise in me.'

There can be few more profitable studies than that of wine, which gives enjoyment both to the student and his or her friends; in research it may take you to foreign lands and generally widen your outlook and your friendly impulses towards the peoples of other countries. Wine is a born ambassador. An intimate knowledge of that once English city, Bordeaux, and friendship with its proud, gay and hospitable citizens, as cosmopolitan as Parisians and as decidedly French in sentiment and fervour, adds permanently to the richness of life. To know and understand and appreciate their wines, the peculiarities and divergences of Médoc, Graves and St Emilion, the ancestry and idiosyncrasies of the *crus classés* of the Médoc and the grapy lusciousness of the hierarchy of Sauternes, is to make you at once *persona grata* in this busy and prosperous centre of viticultural industry. To have driven through the vineyards in an old barouche, as we used to do, or in a smart Delage, as is done nowadays, tasting wines at sundry châteaux as we went along; to have been one of a merry party of *volontaires* (student apprentices) in expeditions and picnics on the green viniferous islands of the muddy Gironde – just like the 'Umber at 'Ull, as the Yorkshirewoman remarked to me once as we entered the river from the Bay of Biscay; to have enjoyed the operas of French and Italian *maestros* and, tentatively, Wagner (I am speaking of fifty years ago) in the palatial renaissance opera-house where, on gala nights, the *beau monde* of Bordeaux would foregather, the men as smartly groomed as the women were fashionably gowned; to have swum in the fast-flowing chocolate-coloured river opposite the Chartrons, as I so often did with Albert Schÿler and his friend Teysonnière; to have dined with my kind patrons *en famille* and cut capers after dinner to the tune of 'Ta-ra-ra-Boom-de-ay' (then the *furore*) or 'See me dance the Polka', when I impersonated Grossmith, are all memories that endear Bordeaux to me in my old age. And all the time to have been gleaning a harvest of knowledge and information that was to be of inestimable value to myself, and I hope to my friends and colleagues, throughout my career in the time-honoured wine trade. Bordeaux was, and I think may still be, the Wine Merchants' University City, and we *alumni* the 'Academicians of Wine', as my friend, Dr Percy Litchfield, would like to have us called.

CHAPTER 8

Côte d'Or Curiosities

Burgundy or Claret. Chablis-Rosé. Decanting. Cannibalism. Tastevin. Successors to Saintsbury. Burgundy at Bordeaux Dinner Party. Registering Taste. Scaling of Alcoholic Strength. Later pre-War Vintages. The Rhône.

It may seem strange, but it is true, that I have never been able to acquire such an intimacy with burgundy as with claret. They are so often classed together and served at table in succession that a knowledge of one would seem to imply or perhaps necessitate a knowledge of the other. There are many far better judges than I am who consider burgundy to be the superior wine. I agree that, taken all over, it displays a more pungent and powerful bouquet than claret, more body and more evident sugar, and a robuster flavour in its masterpieces but not an all-round equal refinement or gentility of quality: its sweetness is not so natural, nor do its humbler denizens show comparable breeding. It is impossible ever to draw a real parallel between the produce of different wine-growing districts. Common burgundy is very common and harsh to the taste, but common claret, the common clarets of years like 1893, 1899 and 1928 were pleasant to drink, soft and supple and satisfying. How diversely dictatorial, too, the human or physical idiosyncrasy is in each one of us! I find red Bordeaux (claret) much easier to digest than red burgundy, and on the other hand I find white burgundy much easier and more agreeable to drink than white Bordeaux. Some of my friends find the exact opposite. So each gets its meed of approbation. The consequence, as far as I am concerned, is that I am much more intimate and on speaking terms with claret than burgundy. In the Côte d'Or the ill-effects of burgundy, curiously enough, do not make themselves felt, and I can enjoy a whole *déjeuner* and dinner, accompanied by a formidable array of burgundy wines, without any forebodings of discomfort to follow. Most wines taste well in their native environments. Of modern burgundy vintages, and by that I mean vintages of this century, I bracket 1904 and 1906 as very fine all through the Côte d'Or, and what was then known as Romanée La Tâche was superb in both years and neither heavy nor stodgy nor heating as so many of the older burgundies were. Then, although there were some attractive wines in 1908 and 1911 (perhaps the latter were unusally dry for burgundy), we had to wait for 1915 for another outstanding vintage, good but disconcertingly variable. This was only to be expected as it was a war baby and many agencies were at work ill-suited to satisfactory development of the wines when young: their later transport across France to the port of embarkation was also hazardous, and many casks arrived over here with the fœtid smell and flavour of canal water and the truth was not in them. We forget, amid the travail and difficulties of the present postwar days (I am now in September 1945), the troubles that had to be encountered and overcome at the close of the First World War. Some Chablis my Dijon firm shipped to us came over in red burgundy casks and had acquired a pinkish tinge of colour. It gave us a lot of trouble, because people in the country began sending it back to us as 'not Chablis'. One well-known London restaurant proprietor, however, put it on his list as 'Chablis-Rosé' and scored a big success. An intelligent use of their inventive faculties would frequently help people through troubles as often as not imaginary. But the 1915 burgundies were on the whole pleasing wines for many years though they hardly fulfilled their early promise. This autumn (1945) I tasted 1915 Nuits, of a good growth, and Clos de Vougeot, and much preferred the former; the latter was acetic. I look upon Clos de Vougeot, as long as it is shared by forty different owners, as the tragedy of the Côte d'Or.

There were many good 1919 wines, especially those bottled and binned in the country of origin. The Bourguignon is a clever and resourceful fellow and, some years ago, he invented a sort of syphon which, in the guise of a thin strand of wire, he could insert between the cork and the glass neck, into a bottle of wine, and, with its aid, extract the heavy sediment which in burgundy is often both plentiful and shifty, like sand. All wines, and certainly all red wines, ought to throw a sediment in bottle, and burgundy does not fail in this duty. There are different ways of dealing with the deposit or sediment in different wines, but careful decanting is the best because it is an operation performed by yourself, and you know quite well that, rather than see a speck of sediment go into your decanter, you will sacrifice a glassful of wine and sometimes a bit over. It is more economical, indeed, to lose a whole glass of wine than ruin, by parsimonious greed, a whole decanterful. Some wine-waiters need reminding, however, that the mere act of pouring wine out of a bottle into a decanter does not of itself clarify the wine! Quite the contrary, the operation requires care, watchfulness and steady handling. I have seen burgundy eat up its own sediment and by doing so increase its sweetness as well as its softness in old age. The attractive, but eccentric, 1895 burgundies were an instance of this and gave a lot of trouble as the majority of them threw a very heavy deposit which, if you turned the bottle upside down and looked through it, you could see floating down like a cloud of soot. Most merchants, I think, emptied their bottles into casks again and rebottled them, and private people probably emptied theirs down the sink and forswore burgundy in the future. I happened to have taken a fancy to an Aloxe-Corton and had put a little of it down in my cellar and, being of a frugal Scottish mentality, instead of throwing it away when it developed this excess of deposit, I left it alone where it was, and, to my gratified surprise some years later, I found that the sediment had almost entirely gone, leaving a mere film round the inside of the bottle. Where had it gone to? There was only one answer – cannibalism! The wine had eaten it up; my remaining bottles were child's play to decant and a pleasure to drink. I always had a warm corner for the 1895s which, without perhaps being great wines, were sweet and amiable all through the gamut.

This is not a textbook or a training manual and, even if I were properly able to do so, I am not going to try to explain the chemical reactions responsible for the above strange phenomenon: it is evidently not so strange as all that in the birthplace of burgundy, and the logical ingenuity of our friends there has, as already mentioned, sought, seemingly with success, to dispel the heavy clouds and help their wine once more to exhibit its bright and sunny nature. On my last visit to the Côte d'Or I dined with Georges Faiveley at his pretty and daintily furnished house in Nuits St Georges. We were a gay party and started off the evening with an *apéritif* in the shape of port; it was served clear. I draw attention to this fact because, as a rule, the port *apéritif* in France, however good a wine in itself, comes to you as thick as pea soup. The series of wines at dinner was well selected and, though I drank my fill of choice growths of 1923, 1915 and back to 1904, I experienced no ill-effects. I kept a copy of the *menu*, as, in its way, it was rather unique with its greetings to me as Chevalier of their pseudo-mediæval Confrérie of the 'Order of Tastevin' – of which Georges Faiveley is the grandest of Grand-Masters – that breathes the self-conscious pride, one might almost call it the boastfulness, the *panache*, of your true Bourguignon. Each of my fellow guests, when he signed his name, added an epigram, a jest or a complimentary word of welcome. I am afraid this much-treasured memento, as well as my gaily illuminated certificate of Tastevinous chivalry, were amongst my many valuable belongings that perished in the historic blitz of 10 May 1941, when Burns Pye and I, and our faithful staff, meeting amid the smoke and stench of the forty-hours' blazing furnace that had been Mark Lane, fared forth into the unknown future, as all other Britons did, determined to carry on somewhere and somehow.

I have drunk older burgundies in this country than any served in the Côte d'Or. Walter Berry had a superb collection of old wines which I think his partner, Hugh Rudd, had found, after the First World War, in Liège where it had been success-fully concealed from the hawk eyes of the Huns. André Simon, too, I remember, produced some exceptionally fine burgundy of the marvellous 'seventy decade when Jean Calvet was amongst his guests, and, to mention one only of amateurs unconnected with the trade, C M Wells, making a cellar where he can, even in his bathroom, they say, has drawn the most fastidious connoisseurs to his table by his knowledge and choice of burgundies. A classical scholar, born athlete and sportsman, entomologist, philatelist, consulted by Kings and commoners, and a contemporary of mine at Dulwich College, Wells has added to these many accomplishments an intuitive, almost inerrable, taste in wines which makes him one of the foremost figures of our time and withal the most retiring and modest. Had he wished he could have penned notes from *his* cellar book that would have equalled or surpassed those of George Saintsbury himself. As a matter of fact, we need a Saintsbury every generation or so. Freshmen and professors alike prefer to read about wines they know or have themselves a chance of cross-examining at the one and only court of appeal. A promising young wine merchant said to me quite recently that he found those companionable *Notes on a Cellar-Book* dull to boredom, since only wines he had heard of but never tasted were mentioned therein. I take the opportunity thus offered of passing this intelligible and potentially constructive criticism on to the younger literary members of the Saintsbury Club, of whom there are not a few; a flagrant example, I fear, of nepotism, but perhaps forgivable.

Sometimes we had burgundy at select dinner parties in Bordeaux: it was usually rather old and choice and followed the most celebrated clarets. A '57 Chambertin was served at one dinner after '75 Mouton Rothschild and '62 Léoville-Lascases for example, and, on another occasion, a '64 Corton after '65 Lafite. At one of the Camille Kirsteins' functions, at Lormont, their pretty place on the cliff overlooking the lights of Bordeaux from the other side of the river, a grand old burgundy was brought round after the usual long list of fine aristocratic clarets, and our host asked us to guess what it was. He gave no hint. Rasmussen, an agent from Denmark, was there and one or two other Continental big noises in the wine trade, but their combined wisdom stumbled heavily on this occasion; I was myself totally at sea. It was Madame Kirstein who rescued us from our dilemma when she said that it must be a burgundy. I forget exactly what its parentage was but she was right. Camille gave us the name of it and said he felt sure his wife would guess it; her own apology for having done so was that she had recognized a *parfum de cire* (smell of sealing-wax) by which her husband had told her she could always distinguish burgundy!! That was at that time what they, nowadays, call 'a new one on me' and I wondered whether some inside information had not inadvertently leaked out before our arrival! Everybody at once began to detect an aura of sealing wax or imagined they did. It is not a bad habit to cultivate some means or method of recognition of wines by simile or resemblance. P G H Fender, who has developed a very discriminating palate since he took up the wine business, always finds a distinct taste of pebbles in the red Graves of Bordeaux and, like many other judges, a taste of truffles in the wines of St. Emilion: he has made as careful a study of subtle differences in wines as he did of the pace and possibilities of a cricket pitch and with corresponding success. I myself invariably recognized a Château Margaux in the old days by a delicious fragrance of boiled rice milk pudding, which was also traceable in its not distant neighbour Brane-Cantenac, and I have already alluded to the unmistakably Oriental-bazaar flavour I have noticed in Clos Fourtet and Cheval Blanc. Vintages, almost more than vineyards, used to have their noticeable characteristics in bygone days but, as I have said before, there seems to be a more general uniformity today. The tasting of wine, and this is applicable to all wines, and not only claret and burgundy, depends largely on the state of health and composure of mind of the taster and the conditions in which he is tasting. And it is just as well that it should be so as, otherwise, some clever tasters would be omnipotent and the rest of us of little or no account. We too have our good days just as they have their bad ones, and we should never be afraid or ashamed to express our findings, or feel it necessary to make fatuous excuses when we are hopelessly wrong. The truly good judge will be able to give a reason for his verdict, whatever it is. This brief dissertation on tasting may, in spite of my efforts, savour somewhat of the textbook, but it is meant as an encouragement to all, amateur and professional, to formulate a personal estimate of a wine, without fear or favour, though some diplomatic or polite turn of phrase may be called for on occasion. Remember the curate and his egg!

Of the fully fledged vintages of burgundy (I observe how the 'egg' provides me with an appropriate designation) I think the 1923 is unquestionably the best since 1906, not the least bit coarse and yet full of wine and flavour, round and sweet, and soft to the palate. This was the vintage that was being shipped in the spring of 1927 when Churchill introduced his famous budget (some wine merchants called it 'infamous') in which he reduced the maximum alcoholic strength of wines termed 'natural' or 'beverage' from 30° proof spirit to 25° (27° for the Dominions, a little bit of patriotic preference!), above which strength all wines had to pay a higher duty. The late Sir Ernest Rutherford and I were roundly denounced by many of our colleagues for supporting this alteration in the dividing line, and particularly by those engaged in the burgundy and Tarragona trades. I acknowledged the hardship to the latter and made very careful inquiries in the Côte d'Or about the former. I was assured that only in very exceptional years would burgundies 'weigh' over the 25° unless they had been '*trop chaptalisés à la cuve*', i.e. had had more than the authorized quantity of sugar spread over the grapes at the time of pressing. This was one of my most convincing arguments in debate so that the laugh was well against me when, on the arrival of the 1923 wines, I lugubriously confessed to our still-protesting committee that nearly all my burgundies just exceeded the limit and would probably have to pay the higher rate of duty. The laughter was loud and hearty, but I am more sure than ever, now that I can look calmly back, that 25° proof spirit is a much truer dividing line between what may be called 'beverage wine' and 'dessert wine' than 30° could have been. But none of these differences of opinion had any effect on the development of the 1923 burgundies which made most satisfactory progress and, if one may judge by a 'Hospice de Beaune', which was on the menu at the 'centenary' dinner of the Saintsbury Club, are not only charming today but give promise of many years more of faithful and acceptable service. There were some light and pretty burgundies of 1924 and none of them ambitious enough to approach the new datum line of 25°! I put a little zero after the wines of 1925 as well! They were poor tackle like the clarets of the same year. I remember Albert Schÿler, in the years 1892–3, often lamenting that he was not a Bourguignon instead of a Bordelais, because, as he said, the burgundy merchants could always claim that the latest vintage was the best ever, while the more truthful

Bordelais could not! As Bacon in his wisdom wrote, 'Kings are not envied but by Kings'.

I began by saying that, however much I might enjoy a good burgundy, I have discovered, by uneasy experience, that burgundy, and particularly young burgundy, has no use for me. Perhaps it is for that reason that, so far, I have not done my duty by the promising vintages of 1928, 1929, 1933 and 1934, all of which appear to me to be good, occasionally very good, but not consistently so; but who can guarantee the future? The 1928s, for instance, are inclined to be what George Saintsbury would have called 'dumb', lacking in animation though full and vinous.

The 1929s are sweet, grapy and attractive, and quite recently I thoroughly enjoyed an Aloxe-Corton, but I am not inclined to place them above, or even on a par with, 1923s, which were of a more noble texture and more representative of the big boastful burgundian at his best. I have always found 1933 and 1934 complementary to each other: both seem to me to be variable and erratic, both produced some very attractive wines and both fell down on occasion disappointingly; 1934 I consider as the better bred, particularly in the fine growths, but inclined to be stiff and standoffish and even hard, faults which good breeding generally in the end overcomes, though it never did in the case of 1911 burgundies or the 1896 clarets. 1933s seem more supple and genial and, in the lower qualities certainly, fuller and sweeter and more likable. Also, let me add, some of the finer growths of 1933 are keen competitors of their successors of 1934. Altogether I feel that burgundy drinkers, like claret drinkers, will have nothing much to complain of for several years to come if 1928s and 1929s, 1933s and 1934s are still obtainable, and they will be luckier still if they can make their own pick of wines. In a gastronomic anthology entitled *We shall eat and drink again*, published by Hutchinson about Christmas 1944, the editors include a 'Song of Burgundy', by William Bliss, which recalled to my mind the festive occasion of the Wine and Food Society's tripartite Burgundy Dinner between the Wars. It was made specially memorable by the presence at it of two well-known Bourguignons, one tall and thin and the other short and fat, who sang, by request and with inimitable humour, a local duet, *'Les Cadets de Bourgogne'*, that added much to the success of the dinner and the merriment of the evening.

It seems quite natural for the tendrils to wander from the Côte d'Or into the Valley of the Rhône, where are to be found the rich attractive red wines of Châteauneuf-du-Pape. One does not often enough come across them, but, in days gone by, I enjoyed more than one bottle of a very excellent representative from a bin which that eminent author and journalist, and equally well-known and reputable wine merchant, Ernest Oldmeadow, used to keep hidden away in the recesses of his cellars in Dean Street; and a remarkable cellar, indeed, it was as those who have had the pleasure of lunching in the panelled room upstairs know well. *Ex Africa aliquid novi* would be far from an inappropriate synonym in connection with the refreshingly unusual fare we there enjoyed; savoury, toothsome courses of native and foreign fish, meats, vegetables, sweets and cheeses of the existence of which one had never, or, in some cases, rarely, heard before, cooked and dished from our host's own *récipés* by a treasure of a *cuisinière*. She was a personage of ample dimensions, not lightly tripping on fantastic toe, but of a countenance that radiated a welcome to the master's guests and beamed with an extensive smile when one expressed approval of her culinary skill. A great woman in her day.

Châteauneuf-du-Pape, it seems to me, is pre-eminently a wine that should be taken at the tide: when quite young it is rough and inclined to be rasping and when it reaches any age it becomes, as a rule, plain and dull and unenticing, but at the right moment it can be exceedingly pleasant and gratifying; that from Old meadow's bin was, but I have not always been so fortunate. I cannot claim to have made any very careful study of Rhône wines, which, besides Châteauneuf-du-Pape, include, amongst others, the better-known, but not much better-known, wines of Hermitage. There is no secret, I think, in the fact that wines from this fertile viniferous valley were much sought after at one time for blending with those of the Burgundy area, which has never been limited entirely to the Côte d'Or, and the Hermitage group, particularly, must have been serviceable for the purpose owing to their fullness of body, strength of vinosity and splendid staying power. Years ago, when I was a young man in business, I came across an old duty-paid price-list of Cock, Reid and Pye, forerunners, in part, of Reid, Pye, Campbell and Hall, and noticed that several of the wines quoted thereon had the word *hermitagé* printed in brackets after their names. In answer to my inquiries, I learned from Reid senior, or Pye senior, I forget which, that they had followed a not unusual procedure in those days of blending some of their lighter-bodied red wines with fine Hermitage to 'bring them up', and had always listed them as such; nor, apparently, had this any prejudicial effect on sales. I suppose they were really performing an operation over here which was, to common knowledge, more frequently carried out in France, and which, so far as my information goes, is no longer permissible or practised. My father bought from a wine merchant, who had missed his market, some dozens of 1864 or 1865 Hermitage which he deposited in our cellars in Mark Lane; for several years, when stock was taken, 'Colonel Campbell's Hermitage' was reported to be occupying a bin which might be more profitably employed; eventually my father distributed it among his partners and friends, and a wonderful wine it was. It must have been quite forty years old at the time, but it was of a dark red colour, superbly full-blooded and big, with a rough-edged sweetness and, as far as I was concerned, of a somewhat indigestible breed. It was a hero, if one might say so, with no pretence to being a gentleman, but there was no question about its being a magnificent figure of a wine. Hermitage, of a still earlier vintage, is very flatteringly mentioned in *Notes on a Cellar-Book*, and praise from such an independent and influential quarter is praise indeed: I will say nothing to detract from it since, as a member of the Saintsbury Club, I rejoice to find that the 'Permanent President' of the Club which was founded in his honour was able to demonstrate so effectively that his love of wine, and literature, was both catholic and articulate.

It is a little surprising to me that red and white Hermitage, and other wines of the Rhône Valley, are not more popular in this country, as they seem capable of filling a gap for those people who are in search of a blood-making beverage and to whom refinement of style and texture is not an essential.

CHAPTER 9

The Wine that is White

White Wines. California and Choate's Advice. Sauternes. Yquem. Klein's Deidesheimer. Montrachet à la Rhin. Ecstatic Description. Rieussec. Finest Dinner Wine List. Finest Luncheon Wine List Dissertation on Brandy.

Like George Saintsbury, I am a 'red wine' man but have taken advantage of many opportunities to appreciate the sometimes seductive witchery of white wines, chiefly French and German. I have even toyed with the white wines of our two viniferous Dominions of Australia (with pleasure) and South Africa (also with pleasure), and also of Hungary (remarkably palatable), Switzerland (somewhat thin and acid), Chile (goodish) and, still earlier, of California. In those days, fifty years ago, the enterprising owners of the 'Big Tree' Brands, so famous for the label showing a charabanc being driven through the gigantic trunk of a tree, used to ship two Californian wines which I constantly found and drank in country hotels. If my memory serves me faithfully they were No. three, called Chablis, and No 12, called Burgundy, and, in spite of these misnomers, both were very good wines without in the least, except perhaps in colour, resembling the white and red wines of Burgundy, whose names they had 'requisitioned'. Californian wines dropped out of the picture when America 'went dry', and I hope that, when they return to our wine-lists, they will have been allowed to profit by the advice of Mr J H Choate, Jnr, a name honoured here as in the USA Mr Choate's words are worthy of repetition; so here they are: 'There is nothing to prevent the American Vintner from eventually producing wines of which the best years' vintages will command prices almost as fabulous as a great Rhine wine or Romanée Conti. No one will ever do this with a wine put out under a foreign geographical name, and thereby self-condemned as an imitation. Individual and Proprietorial names will have to be adopted and made famous by consistent merit. The growers who realize this are playing for an enormous prize.' (Taken from the *Wine & Spirit Trade Review* of 27 March 1936.) These sensible remarks concern others besides the wine-growers in California, including even some of those who draw up wine-lists in this country and whose sense of geographical designation would seem to be hazy and confused. As an example, nothing to my mind surpassed an announcement in, of all places, one of the wine trade papers. It was advertising the wine of Alicante and read 'ALICANTE ALTAR WINE imported direct from Palestine'. It seems to me a far cry from Alicante to the Holy Land but, to be sure, the roots of the vine are votaries of the *wanderlust*. I suppose 'Cheddar Cheese imported from Canada' is equally within the range of possibility, but in this case it must be the maggots that do the travelling.

Sauternes, more often than not spelt erroneously without the final 's', seems to be quite innocently and loosely used in this country as an umbrella for any still white wine from any part of the world, and it hurts my sense of justice to the *Commune* of Sauternes, and the pristine glory of its golden vineyards, to see this done. And, talking of Sauternes, the past generation had opportunities of tasting and discussing the 1869 Ch Yquem, undoubtedly the most exquisitely flavoured sweet white wine of its day, or perhaps of any day, and this generation has, at least I hope it still has, a chance of tasting the 1921 Yquem which offers a resemblance in many ways to its great ancestor but is unlikely to retain its clean, luscious fruitiness for so long. A little lack of uniformity in the way Yquem is sometimes listed may have been observed. There are many who call it, as I do, Château Yquem, but, I think, probably an equally large number call it Château d'Yquem, and sometimes I have seen it listed as Château Y'quem. This last, I think, can be ruled out as meaningless and incorrect, and I do not remember our good historian, M. André Simon, having expressed his opinion on the two former, though he himself writes Yquem as I do. M Féret in '*Bordeaux et ses vins*' (1886), who was my guide in these matters in 1892, certainly calls it Château-Yquem and, in a descriptive note, says '*Le Château-Yquem appartenait autrefois à la maison de Sauvage d'Yquem*', and he goes on to talk of '*Le domaine d'Yquem*' and '*le tonneau d'Yquem*', all of which, while seeming to support my spelling, might also give an excuse to those who fancy the other as an alternative. However that may be, I think there is no doubt that Ch Yquem is *facile princeps* in the domain of natural white sweet wines. German viticulturists have challenged that statement on behalf of one or other of their Palatinate growths. Let us concede at once that a Forster Jesuitengarten, or a Deidesheimer, is sometimes superlatively majestic in the rich saccharinity of its fruit and fabric, but, in my opinion, the best Palatinate will never quite touch the quintessence of sweet refinement possessed by the best Yquem.

I had a friendly discussion on this very point with Otto Klein in Traben-Trarbach and he immediately took steps to convince me of the mistake I made. But his step was faulty. He brought out a superb 1921 Deidesheimer, decorated with all its *trockenbeeren* and *auslesen*, which was admirable, and only my irrepressible optimism led me to feel sure that the 1921 Yquem would beat it. Then Klein, with typical German perfidy, produced the 1920 Yquem which he informed me, on the 'Sez-you' model, was finer than the 1921! Now, the 1920 Yquem was, and, I hope, is, although I have not seen it for many years, an unquestionably fine wine, but it was always completely outclassed by the brilliant qualities of the 1921: it was good enough, however, to run the 1921 Palatinate Goliath so close as to leave us both in doubt as to which was the superior.

There is a marked difference in traditional vinification between French and German white wines, generally, I must confess, to the advantage of the latter as far as my own taste is concerned; there are, however, a few, comparatively few, vineyard proprietors in the Côte d'Or who can and do make really fine and attractive wines in Montrachet and Meursault; still more rare is a white Musigny, though I have already mentioned a quite captivating 1919 that Wells has, or had; and Berry Bros & Rudd had a rather unexpectedly good, though somewhat hard, white Corton, no doubt the Charlemagne. There is also a Clos de Vougeot Blanc but I do not remember having tasted it. It might be very good. I was well taken in by a 1919 Montrachet which Tom Gummer gave us during a luncheon party at Dolamore's office, at which I sat next to Sir Ben Smith, the present Minister of Food: I say advisedly 'the present' as changes of personnel in the political roundabout are so frequent and sometimes so unexpected that one cannot count upon permanency.[1] Wine can be the truest of peacemakers and a sure disseminator of good will: conservative in principle, liberal in diversity, it is genuinely socialist; wine is an ambassador speaking every language and welcome in all countries. Never should monetary expedients be employed to hamper the beneficent flow of wine nor wine itself be subjected to the treatment of a mere pawn in the game of national or international politics. I fear I seem to be addressing Sir Ben as if he were a political meeting! Before I heard what it was, the Montrachet had given me the impression of being a Rhine wine of sorts, but too solid for the Moselle Valley and too much like Burgundy to be a Palatinate. But I was astonished when Gummer told us what it was and later I wrote him a line asking for further particulars. His reply is most interesting and worth quoting in full: 'The wine was Montrachet, Private Reserve, 1919 Vintage, made from selected grapes on the German "Auslese" principle. There were only two hogsheads produced and I was lucky enough to find them, chiefly, I think, because when the old Frenchman who was responsible for their making asked me, at his table, to place the wine, my verdict was a "fine Palatinate". Apparently this was the very thing that he wanted, his ambition being to show that if his countrymen would take the same trouble in grape selection as did the Germans, the results would be the same.'

Of course that is a very far-reaching assertion and makes no allowance for differences of soil and climate and other conditions that influence the style and taste of wines, but it was

---

[1] Sir Ben resigned within a few months of this prophetic comment.

an interesting experiment and the 1919 Montrachet a most attractive and successful produce of Franco-German 'collaboration' if one may say so.

As is well known, the Ch Yquem is vintaged with similar care in the selection of its grapes which are allowed to ripen almost to the extreme pitch of mouldiness and then pressed with amorous solicitude; in my opinion, and in that, I think, of most amateurs, Yquem stands out super-eminent among the white wines of the world, quite unmatched and unmatchable in the refined delicacy of its fragrance, the luscious richness of its flavour and the nutty warmth of its farewell, even if it *has* been 'slightly iced'. The ideal is always to be sought and never to be attained, but, in the realm of white wines, Yquem, at its best, comes as near to perfection as seems possible. We winefolk have sometimes been accused of exaggeration of language when writing about wine but only I fancy by the sort of critic of whom it might be said:

'A primrose by the river's brim,
A yellow primrose was to him,
And it was nothing more.'

What would such an one have said to the *Fifth Symphony* of Sibelius being described as 'that Olympic vision in blue and gold', as it was in a recent issue of the *Observer*, by a writer whose obviously sincere love of beautiful music led him unaffectedly to so colourful a phrase? One is glad to revel in and applaud it as well as the dulcet nordic harmonies and Russian-ballet exuberances, themselves so dear to Sibelius.

Ch Yquem is not the only fine wine of the Sauternes area,

le pays de Sauternes; Châteaux Vigneau, Rieussec, Peyraguey, Filhot, Guiraud, Coutet, Climens, Suduiraut and La Tour-Blanche, to mention only some of the best-known, produce delicious, fine, mellifluous wines in their good years, and in some vintages one may prefer one or other of them even to the mighty Yquem itself, particularly, perhaps, in recent years. Sauternes, it seems to me, are wines of which to drink one glass, and that preferably at dessert as a *bonne bouche*, in lieu of the habitual glass of port. To drink more at a sitting is, in my experience, apt to upset the complacency of the inner man, though I am sorry to say, or was sorry to say soon after the occasions, that I have frequently been led by the seductiveness of the wine or the blandishments of my host to break this golden rule. I have seen a man and woman, an unsophisticated looking young couple, share a bottle of 1921 Ch Yquem through a whole dinner. True, they did not mix it with anything else, but I would like to have been able to inquire how they felt next morning. White wines should always be served cold, not necessarily iced, but indisputably COLD.

Ch Filhot has always been one of my favourite Sauternes, perhaps because in so many years it is rather less luscious than most of the others, of which I find Coutet – a Barsac-Sauternes – is more often than not the most blatantly sweet. Filhot is owned, as Yquem is, by the family of de Lur Saluces and is equally cherished. I always retain a very pleasant recollection of its 1914 vintage as I used to think that, if all Sauternes were like that, rather light but full of flavour, sweet but not extravagantly, nutty and unspoilt by that sulphurous cloying aftertaste, which, in my opinion, often characterises them to their detriment, I would be a drinker of Sauternes. Of the others I have happiest recollections of the Ch Rieussec, which is uniformly of above-par quality even for a *grand cru* of Sauternes. This château is situated in Fargues, a *commune* which together with Barsac, Bommes and Preignac comes into *le pays de Sauternes*. At the head of what I have always considered to be the finest series of Bordeaux wines served at any dinner of which I was one of the lucky partakers, I find, in my notes, the name of Rieussec. The dinner took place in Bordeaux at Christmastide 1892 in the house of the Camille Kirsteins, and I apologize to M André Simon and the council of the Wine and Food Society for being unable to supply particulars of the edibles which, however, they may rest assured were worthy of the succession of heroic wines. This is the list: 1869 Ch Rieussec, 1877 Ch Brane-Cantenac, 1875 Ch Cheval Blanc, 1875 Ch Brane-Cantenac, 1875 Ch Mouton Rothschild, 1874 Ch Haut-Brion, 1871 Ch Pape-Clément, 1871 Ch Mouton Rothschild, 1871 Ch Latour, 1864 Ch Larose-Bethmann (Faure), 1859 Ch Mouton Rothschild. I see I put a star indicating '*exquis*' against the '69 Rieussec, '75 Brane, '75 Mouton, '74 Haut-Brion and '71 Latour, but I imagine it must have been consummate cheek on my part, with my immature expertise at that time, to have registered in black and white what I can now justifiably consider to have been a very happy selection. Brandy followed with the coffee but I have no record of what it was.

Just about thirty years later, in 1921, in André Simon's own office, and in company with him and the two Rendleshams, and others, we liquidated the following unsurpassable luncheon list, which I think must have been included in André's *Tables of Content*, but have not my copy of this appetizing volume with me: 1868 Ch Yquem, 1875 Ch La Lagune, 1875 Ch Larose-Sarget, 1875 Ch Branaire, 1864 Ch Léoville-Barton, 1864 Ch

Lafite, 1874 Ch Haut-Brion (magnum), 1871 Ch Lafite, 1847 Port (magnum) – Cockburn, I think – 1808 Cognac, Denis-Mounié. On a previous page I have alluded to the unusual but carefully considered sequence in which some of the wines were served. As the perfect liqueur to wind up a good dinner, fine cognac has no rival. Its spirit, distilled from the juice of the grape, is soft, fragrant, clean and dry. It seems to me a pity to colour and sweeten it in imitation of an entirely different class of liqueur which may have its appeal on certain occasions and in certain company. I say nothing against these other liqueurs; I have enjoyed them from time to time and once helped two stalwarts to empty a bottle of green Chartreuse at a sitting, returning to my office stool after it fit and well! But for faithful and beneficial service brandy stands alone. In addition to their standard marks, such as 'three stars', 'vsop', and so on, most shippers have sent us, from time to time, straight vintage lots and, without going too far back, we can all remember the pale colour and beautiful quality of Hine, Hennessy, Martell, Delamain and others, either in 1900, 1904 (1905 Martell, excellent), 1906, 1911, 1913, 1914, and even at this early date, 1922. I have also tasted younger. Most of these vintage brandies were shipped in cask, at the age of one year, into British bonds where they would mature more slowly, and often more satisfactorily, than they would abroad, and were bottled about twenty-five to thirty years later. I often say that 1808 Denis Mounié was the finest of fine brandies I ever tasted, but I believe that a little while after the particular luncheon mentioned above Francis Berry put up another somewhat younger *fine champagne* which Rendlesham the Second conceded was still more perfect. I query.

Judging from the above symposial array I do not think Mark Lane, as we knew it before the Blitz, had much cause to bow the knee either to the Allées des Chartrons or to St James's Street.

CHAPTER 10

A Homily on Graves

Some White Bordeaux. Vogue in Graves. Carbonnieux. Bordeaux Policy.
Red Queen *v* White Queen.

For those who like and wish to drink white Bordeaux, but find
Barsac and Sauternes generally too sweet, and ordinary and
unidentifiable Graves too insipid, or, as I do, too nauseating, I
would suggest an excursion into the riparian vineyards lying on
either side of the Garonne between Bordeaux and Sauternes;
and, if I were asked to particularize, I would mention the districts of Langoiran, Podensac, Cérons, Loupiac and Ste. Croix
du Mont. The worst of generalization of that sort is that it is
almost always bound to be unjust, and, because I have been
frank enough to know and to say that the ordinary white Graves
which one comes across in private houses and elsewhere do not
appeal to me, I would not like to seem, presumptuously, to condemn all the white wines of the Graves district. I have already
mentioned the white wine of Haut-Brion, which is of distinguished quality, and many other vineyards in the Graves produce both red and white wines whereof normally I, personally,
prefer the red: but the white are sometimes very good. For the
last fifty years there has indeed been a notable *crescendo* in the
public taste for what I might call identifiable white Graves,

that is, those with a name or trade mark which identifies them with a recognized proprietor or shipper. Château Carbonnieux is perhaps the best known, but it has many rivals to be found in the copious holdall I have envisaged in the preceding sentence, among them the Ch Olivier, La Flora Blanche, Dry Royal, Clos du Cardinal, Rosechatel, Goutte d'Or and many others. I think I am possibly in a better position than anyone else now living to trace the origins of this successful enterprise on the part of the Bordeaux shippers. It was while I was over there in 1892–93 that the claret trade was feeling the full effects of the ravages of the phylloxera, and the decrepit mildewed aftermath that overshadowed the '80 decade. Many a time did my friend Albert Schÿler tell me that the taste for claret would soon be a thing of the past and Bordeaux a ruined city: pictures of Troy and Carthage and ill-fated Pompeii crashing over the heads of their devoted citizens were conjured up, and the outlook for a young man just going into the Bordeaux business seemed bleak and unpromising. One day, however, Albert called me into his office and asked me to taste some white wine that the firm had just bought. It was very good and happened to be the 1884 Ch Carbonnieux: this vineyard, situated at Léognan in the Graves, produced both red and white wines, and I had never previously heard of its existence. In addition to the 1884, my friends had also bought the 1889 and contracted for the purchase of the 1891 and following vintages for a period of years. Soon after this, Albert produced an ornate label in white and gold, a distinguished looking capsule, also in white and gold, and, with instinctive genius, a small neck ticket bearing the mystic words on it, 'This bottle should be slightly iced' – a real brain-wave at the time. Then he turned to me and asked if

I thought we could sell the Château Carbonnieux in England and I unblushingly said 'yes'. That it turned out to be a success was to be proved by the number of white Graves, similarly 'got up', with neck tickets and all, that came scrambling one after another on to the British market, until it was forgotten that there was ever such a thing as a new creation or ever a man of an inventive and adventurous imagination like my friend Albert Schÿler. In my capacity as 'English clerk' in the office of Schröder and Schÿler & Cie I spent several weeks writing (there was no typewriter then) scores of letters, to all parts of the world, extolling the virtue and beauties of the new luminary in the Bordeaux firmament, and, in doing so, I made full use of M. Féret's information that: '*En 1741, ce château passa dans les mains des Bénédictins de l'Abbaye de Sainte-Croix de Bordeaux. Depuis cette époque les vins blancs de Carbonnieux ont joui d'une réputation européenne; la Turquie surtout, en dépit du Coran, les recherchait beaucoup. Pour leur faire franchir les barrières de la Sublime-Porte, les Bénédictins, dit-on, étampaient leur vin: "Eau minérale de Carbonnieux".*'

The contract between our friends and the owners continued up to the close of the First Great War when the latter, taking advantage of the War legislation permitting them to do so, terminated the contract and demanded a price for its renewal which our friends considered to be exorbitant. We supported the views of our friends who decided, very wisely, to break fresh ground, buy their white Graves wines from any other vineyard or vineyards they chose in the district and ship under a registered name. Hence Rosechatel, which became an instantaneous success for which I claim a small share of credit as the one who gave it its rather attractive name. I wonder whether the partiality for these White Queens will have survived the War or whether the Red Queens will again assert their claims? In my opinion, the Bordeaux shippers made a mistake in sending us crude young red wines, at extravagant prices, after the First World War and pushing their more commonplace cheap white wines on to the British market. These latter have many rivals, coming pre-eminently from Germany, but also from our own Dominions, and the Balkans and elsewhere, and may be subject to the fads and fancies of fickle and fluctuating fashions, whereas claret, and I mean thereby red Bordeaux, stands without a rival in the world. It is possible that the hustling mode of life in these present days, the exiguousness of flat accommodation, and the anxiety to ensure sales for quick consumption with a minimum of trouble, have produced a demand for wines that can be served at table immediately and undecanted; it cannot be denied that these light white beverage wines, whether they come from France or Germany, or any other viticultural country, are, as a rule, much pleasanter to drink when they are young and fresh than when they have acquired a mawkish bottle taste or, as so often happens, developed an obvious but elusive deposit that may cloud the wine and vitiate its flavour. The Germans appear to me to have been cleverer than the French in subjugating this latter tendency in white wines, owing perhaps to difference in the national laws of vinification. The fact remains, however, that the slogans of the 'quick turnover', the 'nimble sixpence', 'make hay' and *carpe diem*', have or should have no place in the aesthetic domain of any art, and certainly not in what M. André Simon has rightly called the 'Art of Wine'.

As I recall the words of that long-headed Scot, Andrew Bonar Law, uttered in a different setting, 'It will not, I think, be due to irresistible natural laws, it will be due to the want of human wisdom,' I cannot but feel convinced that my Bordeaux friends, not lacking in human wisdom, must realize that claret, the wine which has won for them a warm place in the hearts of winelovers, will for ages to come maintain them in that secure and well-merited haven. I hope, on the other hand, that nothing I have written will seem to have sprung from a desire to decry French white wines, but I am a red wine, and not a white wine, enthusiast though I enjoy a glass of either, and, if good, of both, in season.

CHAPTER 11

'Mitropa'

Wines of Jura and Dalmatia. The Rhine. Budapest and the Blue Danube. Tokay and Madeira. Hocks, Moselles and Saintsbury.

Warner Allen, I think, it is who, in one of his beautifully penned books on wine, likens the white wine of the Jura to fine sherry. I should mention, too, *en passant*, that Lady O'Malley (Ann Bridge), in what I consider to be her best book so far, *Illyrian Spring*, similarly compares a certain Dalmatian wine, with a breakneck name, to the finest sherry. I was very disappointed with the former, when Douglas West gave me a chance of tasting it, and would much have preferred an unpretentious fino sherry; and with the latter I was even more disappointed when I tasted it in the O'Malley's country home in Surrey. Possibly the bottle had not recovered from its precarious journey as there was a lack of integration about it that no respectable sherry, let alone the finest, would have deigned to admit or even possess. I believe the Jura wine produces or throws up a scum on its surface in the spring of the year in the same mysterious way that the Fino *soleras* do in Jerez: there it is called 'flowering' but that is a euphemistic description of its appearance. At the same time the *solera* would not be considered normally healthy if the flower, *la flor*, did not surge annually to the surface of the wine in its cask. I agree with Saintsbury that women sometimes have remarkably good palates and a taste as correct as can be desired, but they have rarely the knowledge or the training to enable them to express their discrimination between wine and wine. The 'Art of Wine' is not yet part of the educational curriculum for young people, boys or girls, and the latter are not often given the same opportunities for making good the deficiency that the former are accorded when school-days are done. Some people, women particularly, may disdain to have any contact with the 'trade in alcoholic liquors', but they delight to be looked upon, in their social circle, as good cocktail mixers! How much better for them, now and hereafter, to study to enjoy their equally companionable, and much more gratifying, glass of wine.

One cannot but feel anxious about the fate of German wines with the triple control of the Rhine resulting from the allied defeat of Germany. I have myself, during my recent chairmanship of the Wine and Spirit Association, put forward proposals that the wine industry of the Rhineland should be placed under the charge of a small commission representative of France, Britain, Belgium and Holland, in order to safeguard the cultivation of the vineyards, which are undoubtedly of great value, and superintend the making of the wines which are a source of health and delight to many and could be valuable also to the account for reparations. It would be a sad pity, I think I used the word 'crime', were vineyards that produced such universally esteemed wines to be allowed to go out of cultivation owing simply to a spirit of revenge or indifference.

For many years, even after I had entered the wine trade, I disliked German wines. I found Moselles deficient and acid and Hocks heavy and heady. I need not say that more intimate acquaintance has entirely changed my estimation. When they are young I find keen enjoyment in the light green 'deficient' 'acid' wines of the Moselle, and its tributaries the Saar and the Ruwer, and, when they are older, I enjoy, but perhaps not quite so unreservedly, and in more limited quantity, the 'heavy and heady' wines of the Rheingau and Rheinhesse, some of which have no superiors of their kind; and, when they are older still, I can enjoy and linger over, with a friend (the greatest enjoyment of all), a glass of the fine Palatinate wines to which I have alluded elsewhere. When traversing the Rhine country I found that many bottles of Moselle would be consumed at a sitting without raising a blush, but it struck me that their bottles were unusually small! Otto Klein was a big fellow and a great sportsman, and his conversation was gamy and entertaining. He took a great fancy to my son, Lorne, when we were there together, and later invited him to accompany himself and Frau Klein to Berlin. Little did he imagine to what extent and in what manner Lorne would distinguish himself in the conflict with Germany a few years later. A rather attractive 'cup' finished our evenings at the Kleins' house; it consisted of sparkling Rheinwein, called 'Champagne', well iced, with fresh peaches or nectarines soaking in it; these you stabbed with a prong so that their sweet juice mingled with the fizz and, if I may say so, gave it a flavour. But at one or two o'clock in the morning, after a day's climbing among the hot slaty vineyards it was very refreshing. It reminded me not a little of the Bola of wild strawberries, drowned in white wine, that my wife and I so much enjoyed in Budapest, to the accompaniment of strangely alluring gipsy music, wild and weird, when our kind and courteous Hungarian hosts entertained us in one of the softly illumined palaces on 'the island' until far into the night. On my wife's birthday too the Hungarian gallants presented her with a wonderful bouquet of field flowers. Strauss himself, no less than Brahms and Liszt, came to life in those, to us, novel and fascinating surroundings, and the melodious strains of *Wein, Weib und Gesang* on the Blue Danube itself, were no longer merely a figment of the imagination. Alas! that the Danube is only blue in the eyes of the poet and composer. I have seen the Thames look more blue from the Terrace of the House of Commons. On the terraces of the Danube we breakfasted with Mr William Byass, best beloved and respected *doyen* of the wine trade, and his handsome lady, who died, much regretted, during the invasion days of the War; and there, too, was Francis Berry, with his keen eye for the antique, and Charles Moss and Arbuthnot Lane, the noted independent medico, who told me it was he who had persuaded George Lansbury to create a Lido on the Serpentine. He was a tremendous advocate of sunbathing, and liquid paraffin and good brandy: No! not all mixed. More people die, said he, from eating too much meat than from drinking too much alcohol. He was well over eighty when he, too, passed away during the War. I found the Hungarian white wines very palatable though perhaps lacking in any marked distinction. Bottled in Rhinewine bottles, one instinctively criticized them from a Rhinewine angle which proved a little too severe on them. They went well however with the *paprika déjeuner* which Oldmeadow gave us at a restaurant overlooking an open-air swimming pool, the placid surface of which was disturbed by an occasional huge wave electrically controlled. This was sunbathing at its best during those warm June days, but we had no time to participate. The Hungarian red wines were relatively nothing like so good as the white, though possessing equally unpronounceable names; and Tokay, the wine of Emperors, which I had looked forward to tasting on its native heath, was most disappointing. What was served to us was unlikely to have come from the Imperial cellars but it was very poor stuff, mawkish and vapid, with an entire absence of a polite farewell. I think Tokay may resemble Madeira which, I always consider, must be very old to be really enjoyable. Fine old Madeira, such as that to which the late Sir Stephen Gaselee used to treat us, is among the most delectable wines I know, stately, precise, neither too sweet nor too dry, combining the fruitiness of fine old vintage port with the nutty finish of a fine old amontillado sherry. I smack my lips as I recall to mind the 1792 Bual and the Sercial da Donna Isabel Esmeralda da Camara that we have had at the Saintsbury Club. Tokay never gave me anything like so much pleasure though it may have helped me to recover from a bad attack of bronchitis not many months ago. My friends, Berry Bros and Rudd, with characteristic kindness, sent me a bottle of Tokay Essens which is said to possess extraordinary virtue in revivifying the moribund. Although I was by no means *in extremis* my doctor added the Tokay to my diet and, well, here I still am. The recovery was complete. Griffith, or 'G' as he is better known, and the Tokay had done it. 'G' used to tell a story of a colleague of his in the medical profession who received a telegram from one of his clients which ran 'my wife is at death's door, please come at once and pull her through'. He said it was a chestnut but it was a good one. Most stories of that sort must perforce be chestnuts!

I have said little about hocks and moselles for the very good reason that I have not made so careful a study of them as, for instance, I have of Bordeaux wines, and I hesitate to pronounce views or reflections which might mislead those searchers after reliable information who are kind enough to read me. This has never prevented me however from following in the footsteps of Wordsworth's idler who, with some worldly wisdom, was

'Contented if he might enjoy
The things which others understood.'

I fear it has been sheer idleness and an instinctive horror of the Teuton tongue that have combined to prevent me from recording in my notes the names, sometimes long, guttural, double- or treble-barrelled names, of the many hocks and moselles I have shared and enjoyed with good friends. George Saintsbury dismissed these wines with an almost disdainful wave of the hand and casual, rather caustic, reflections on those who produced them. I think they may have disagreed with him owing to a certain concealed acidity, particularly in those made on the banks of the Moselle and its tributaries, the Saar and Ruwer, and that he did not trust them. For my own part I look upon them as offering some of the best and most enjoyable of the white wines of the world. I prefer them young, and they must be served cold, whether young or old. All the good moselles can be drunk when they are two years old, and most of them are pretty well past their best when they are ten. 1937s are in their prime today. 1921 however, that *annus mirabilis* for white wines, produced wines throughout the valleys of the 'Castled Rhine' and the Moselle which were quite exceptional, and many of those growths, which normally should be dead and forgotten, are still alive and well today. I apologize to Horace

Vachell, who prophesied this destiny for the 1921 vintage when he wrote about it in a pamphlet at the end of 1922 or beginning of 1923, for having rather tersely questioned his so confident assumption, when reviewing his pamphlet in one of the wine trade newsprints. He was right, however, and I absurdly wrong, as so often before – and since. It was my ignorance of the rapid growth towards maturity which characterizes these wines: the 1893, which was the vintage I knew best at that time, had not, in my recollection, developed with such speed, and it only confirms Vachell's verdict on the remarkable quality of the 1921s that so many of them are still fresh and good to drink.

Reverting to Saintsbury's strictures on German wines, I fancy the Rhinelanders themselves make an intimate and easily accessible knowledge of their wines more difficult by too elaborate a panoply of minute distinctions. When you find that a hock or moselle does not echo your recollection of what it was like the last time you drank it, and ask why, you are met with explanations, no doubt correct but confusing to the uninitiated, that introduce the words *auslese* or *spätlese*, or *beeren* in varied forms, *goldbeeren*, *trockenbeeren*, etc., all indicating grape-selection in one single vineyard in one vintage year. This system of viticulture and vinification is very praiseworthy, very thorough and very German, and to the expert and connoisseur, the Gus Mayer, the Charles Hasslacher, the Hugh Rudd, unquestionably interesting, but it may be tantalizing and perplexing to the George Saintsbury and others whose lack of familiarity with, and insufficient knowledge of, the precise technique, engenders doubts and scepticism. There are potential virtues in simplicity.

I have not had a chance of tasting any of the War years' wines of the Rhineland, but I have enjoyed many of pre-war years since the excellent 1920s and unique 1921s, none perhaps more than those of 1934, 1935 and 1937, and particularly these last and youngest; but then I have already said that I prefer them young, though I confess the prickle of fermentation in some (cleverly 'admired' as *spritzig* by the Germans) does not appeal to me.

CHAPTER 12

The Tendrils Roam: East, West and South

Some Dominion Wines. Nomenclature. White Port and Royal Artillery.
W G Grace. Alsace. Colmar Fête du Vin. Wines of Chile. Wine for the
Many. Wines of Argentina.

I am not sure that Tokay comes under the heading of white
wine but it butted in very conveniently in front of the Rhine
wines and, having said all about it that I wished to, I pass on
to other less pretentious, but equally imperial, vinous delicacies. I was introduced to Paarl Amber, a white beverage wine
from South Africa, by Mr Charles Stuart who at one time was
Headmaster of St Dunstan's College, a colleague of Professor
Henry Armstrong, who was on the Governing Board, and the
introducer of the 'heuristic method' of teaching science in
schools. I found the Paarl Amber clean and dry, palatable and
pleasant to drink. Here is a wine that has no need to stigma-
tize itself as an imitation of French or German or any other
European prototype, and I am sure there must be scores of
others fully entitled to do likewise, to the great and lasting
advantage of the South African vineyards and the reputation of
South Africa as a wine-producing – and exporting – country.
I have added the word 'exporting' because an impression was
prevalent some time ago that the Afrikanders kept their best

wines for themselves and exported the others. I cannot think that that not unfriendly criticism, if justified at the time, holds good any longer. In Australia the custom must have been just the reverse, since, in a blue book issued officially by the Australian Wine Board some years before the War, I saw that the percentage of their own domestic wines consumed by the inhabitants of the sub-continent was infinitesimal, so much so indeed that one was almost tempted to argue that, if the quality of the wines was not good enough to make the Australians themselves wine-drinkers, there could be little expectation of their success with peoples who were in the habit of drinking the well-established wines of Europe. In spite of my attempts to be impartial, I must confess that, in my younger days, I found that practically all Australian beverage wines, white or red, affected, somewhat adversely, my organs of assimilation. I used to ascribe this to various causes, their immaturity, over-robust constitution, the addition of raw brandy at the time of shipment, faults of vinification, mass production and so on: in the private cupboard, at 25 Mark Lane, we had wines, from a leading Australian shipper, which had been in bottle twenty years and more and had never overcome that inability to pass the standard of a perhaps too delicate digestion. But they were not alone in this: I have already attributed to French Burgundy the same sort of drawback!

I think the First World War gave Australian viticulturists their chance and that they seized it with the same tenacity and determination to succeed as that exhibited by their compatriots in other fields of competitive activity and skill, notably cricket and tennis. The fact remains that, partially on patriotic grounds, partially owing to fiscal advantages, and, mainly because of a very pronounced improvement in quality, the wines of Australia have advanced in public favour more than ever before. Not long ago, Cuthbert Burgoyne gave me a white Australian beverage wine, in what looked like a hock bottle, called Springvale, a most pleasing light wine and one worthy of so pretty and so appropriate a name. Why should not the Hunter River, and the happy valley where Springvale flourishes make as great a renown for themselves as the Douro and the Moselle have for themselves? As their importers know, the chief fault I have ventured to lay at the door of our Dominion wine exporters has been their imitative nomenclature: it has shown a lack of imagination that was not to be expected from young and virile communities. A member of the Legislative House of South Africa went so far as to claim the right of using, as the name for South African sparkling wine, 'the good old English word Champagne'!

If Portugal insists, with every reason, on the monopoly of the word Port, seeing that the wine so-called comes from O Porto (the port), it should not be beyond the faculty of countries that produce wine of the character and in the manner of port wine to find a better name for their produce than 'sweet', which is unimpressive and incurs the extra disadvantage of their beverage wines being promiscuously termed 'Dry' – often a grave misnomer. Burgoyne told me he had once made efforts to induce the Australians to call their 'port-type' wine Aust, but without success, and now the word is used for other commodities than wine and is no longer available. It seems a pity. In one of the examination papers that André Simon and I set the students of the Wine Trade Club's educational campaign some years ago we posed the question, 'What is Burgundy?'

We received many first-rate answers and some less so, but the answer that impressed itself most upon us came, I think, from a clerk in a country wine-merchant's office and was to the effect that 'Burgundy is a red wine from Australia but there is also a Burgundy that comes from France'! Even the South African parliamentarian could hardly beat that! But this is one of my numerous digressions and only excusable on the grounds of a sincere desire to see Australian and South African wines, which I envisage as taking an important share in the carrying on of the wine trade of this country in the future, established upon the surest foundations and flying their own flags and not those of foreign, even if friendly, nations.

And speaking of port wine, there is, of course, a white port, made after the similitude of red port but from white grapes in *lieu* of red, and, as a 'Red Wine' man, that makes all the difference to me. I am no lover of white port unless it be of the very finest quality. But I have at least one happy memory in connection with it. The Royal Artillery Mess at Shoeburyness had an enviable reputation, not only for gunnery but also for cricket and some priceless white port. When I went down there with I Zingari [a nomadic cricket club with no home ground, founded 1845], my skipper, Major W E Hardy, a Gunner himself, who has long since joined the great majority, whetted my appetite with tales of the Mess's famous cellar. Yes, I did enjoy the white port to the entrancing strains of Gilbert and Sullivan and other suitable music, played by the R A Band in far from austere or warlike surroundings. If I remember rightly, P F Hadow, G F Vernon, A D Wauchope and I had to run like the very mischief to beat the clock on the second afternoon and score a win against most sporting and chivalrous hosts. Lovely cricket, lovely days! Field-Marshal Lord Milne, himself Master-Gunner, tells me that he thinks they still have white port in the Shoebury Mess and, at one Depot or another, still some pre-war wines in their cellars. And he said it with obvious relish! I hope, for his sake, that some super-excellent '23 burgundy may have escaped the ravages of time and other intruders, as he is a lover of burgundy. Talking of cricketing days reminds me, not inopportunely, that W G Grace, with whom I played a good deal on the picturesquely situated old Crystal Palace wicket, always drank Irish whisky in preference to Scotch when he got the chance, and never seemed a penny the worse, which to a Scotsman is almost incredible. 'W G' was always the centre of any cricket field on which he was playing, whether it was Lord's, Bristol or the Crystal Palace, and he knew it. One day London County was playing against Oundle Rovers, for whom 'W G' Junior (or, as he was generally called, 'Jun') was playing as a master at the school. 'Jun', a grim, drab, fellow, wearing specs, who was a Cambridge Blue – unkind people said 'by courtesy' – had played a remarkably fine innings, hitting the bowling of his father and others of us to all the boundaries: when he got to 99, old 'W G' put himself on to bowl, and, as was our wont in those days, sent him a full toss wherewith to make it a century; but 'Jun' hit the air and the ball hit the wicket and 'Jun' was out clean bowled. I think the Doctor was as annoyed with himself as with his son:

'Ah me! how seldom see we sons succeed
Their father's praise, in prowess and great deed.'

I hope the solace was soothing whether it was 'Irish' or 'Scotch'.

I have made no allusion yet to Alsatian wines, but it is quite on the cards that they may have to deputize, to some extent, for German hocks and moselles until the last wisps of the fog of war have been dissipated. One always surmised that the identity of these wines was merged and lost in that of their bigger and more powerful rivals: little was heard of them until a few years ago when the ethics of self-determination, a confounding ideology, began to penetrate to the vinelands. The wines of Alsace are good and much resemble in style and flavour those produced by the vineyards of their better-known northern neighbours on the Rhine. What a tremendous accessory to the peace of Europe would be the creation of a buffer, vine-occupied, state, under the name of the Rhineland, between France and Germany! Wobbling statesmen failed to seize the opportunity after the First World War: will they fail again after a victorious close to the Second World War has, providentially, offered them a second chance?

It was at the time when the annual French Wine Fête was being held in Colmar a year or two before war broke out that my wife and I accompanied a small party, organized by André Simon, to Alsace and struck what to me was entirely fresh ground. We were a merry party, and, whether we were supposed to represent the Wine and Food Society or not, we were fairly well qualified to do so. Besides André and his wife were the Dowager Lady Swaythling (less dowager-looking than any other Dowager I ever saw), Ernest Oldmeadow, Vyvyan Holland and James Laver, who proved himself to be almost as fluent a speech-maker in French as he is in English. Instead of being crowded into some stiff and noisy cosmopolitan hotel we were all comfortably parked on private houses, my wife and I finding ourselves most hospitably welcomed by M and Madame de Retz, in Mulhouse, of whose kindness we retain very happy recollections. M. de Retz superintended the important potash mines that lie hidden beneath the battle-scarred French soil and serve to enrich the productivity of the soil of the world. Needless to say, we descended one of the mines and experienced the overwhelmingly heavy warmth of the infernal regions: but that, again, is another story. The Rhine seemed very narrow near Mulhouse and to be spanned by a bridge that could not have barred any serious attempt to cross it. This, in truth, was the disputed borderland, and it required no abnormal gift of imagination or intuition to sense a cross-blend of different peoples. The whole atmosphere, the style of the buildings, the look of the inhabitants, their bilingual dialect and its intonation, more teuton I thought than gallic, the public notices and names of places, shops and goods, helped one to realize how near the fateful line of demarcation must be and how commingled the blood of this martyred people. May we hope that the days of suffering are forever ended and that 'la dernière classe' will become a rose-petalled legend instead of a realistic poignant incentive to revenge. From Mulhouse we went to Colmar for the gay multicoloured vintage procession, representative of different wine centres of France, in which M Lebrun, the last President of the Third Republic, drove. The inevitable and not unwelcome déjeuner d'honneur took place in what I presume was the Town Hall, crowded to capacity. Here I was happy to meet a number of friends from various parts of France and, squeezed between two officers of high degree, drink my share of a number of different wines, local and other, donated, I have no doubt, by the makers whose names, in prominent glittering letters, figured on the labels. To parody Dean Inge, the 'gloomy dean', one might say that wine, like literature, flourishes best in some surroundings when it is half a trade and half an art! It would be quite impossible to stage a wine festival on such a large and democratic scale in this country, since, unfortunately, Providence has not endowed us with a viticultural climate nor an indigenous wine-producing potential; but in Colmar it was very picturesque and in jollity and good humour compared favourably with our own somewhat less highly organized and pretentious Harvest Home. We visited the chief centres of the local wine industry, those steep narrow villages, of which Riquewihr was the most fascinating with its quaint diversely built and coloured dolls' houses and chalets clambering up the main, apparently single, street. André Simon suggests that it is because the names of the picturesque Alsatian villages are so difficult to pronounce that the owners of the local wines call these by the names of the species of grapes from which they are made, as for instance Traminer 1937 or Riesling 1937, adding the name of the proprietor for the sake of identification. This is an object lesson to those makers of wine in other parts of the world who imagine they can only market their products under imitative appellations. If I remember rightly, the Cabernet, Malbec, Pinot, and other species of grape with pretty and distinctive names, have already been used to label some few of the wines we see in this country: there is much to be gained by an extension of the practice. I hope we shall never see for instance, Liebfraumilch or Berncastler Doctor from Alsace! which pious aspiration reminds me of the very old story of the man who went into a City restaurant and asked for a fried sole and some Liebfraumilch: when the waitress brought the sole she apologized for not being able to bring the Liebfraumilch as they only had cheddar and gorgonzola in the house.

And, talking of girls calls to mind another tour we had with André Simon and his wife, one Easter, shortly prior to the First World War and just after the son of an old friend of ours, W H Garrett, had been accidentally killed in a football match at Périgueux. We took Garrett for a motor tour to try and cheer him up, and Peter Lawless, who was later to be sports correspondent of the *Morning Post* – and had already played rugger for England, if I remember rightly – and my eldest boy, Lorne, were also with us. Cars used to be tired out (no joke intended!) in those days if they did a hundred miles in the twelve hours, and for our three days' tour we decided not to do more than hover round the Sussex coast. One night we came to the White Hart Hotel at Lewes, booked our rooms and ordered dinner. Seeing Graham's 1887 Port on the wine-list, André ordered a bottle out of compliment to me. The girl, a good stolid-looking local lass, brought the bottle up very carefully and placed it lying down on the sideboard while she got out a decanter and a corkscrew. 'I'll decant it,' said Simon making for the sideboard: 'No you won't', retorted the young woman. 'I'll do it myself much better than you can'. And, not knowing in what august presence she stood, she decanted it splendidly, much to André's astonishment and delight, our amusement and the subsequent general enjoyment. That port, thank goodness, was not a white wine, far from it, brilliantly ruby and, as such, is an interloper here, for whose interloping I must offer my excuses.

Chile is a country about whose wines we hear and know

little in Britain but I believe they meet with considerable favour in the United States. The Chileans, by nature perhaps dilatory and happy-go-lucky, have gone about viticulture and wine-making in a very businesslike way, just as in the old days the Californians did. They selected the Pinot vine, which has made the reputation of the Côte d'Or, and, from varieties of it, they produce both red and white wines. I am sure we could do with very much larger quantities of cheap, sound and attractive table wines than at present we seem likely to be able to get from the European Continent and our overseas Dominions all put together, and competition is a first-rate promoter of excellence. Quite recently I have had an opportunity of tasting some good middle-class wines from Chile, both red and white, and was much taken by the quality, particularly that of the white wines which were bright-eyed, clean and dry, with a most pleasing flavour which I should imagine derived from the white Pinot grape. The red wines were clean to the palate but lacking in body, and, perhaps, a trifle too neutral in flavour; but, on the whole, I was favourably impressed with both the red and white.

There are those who assert that we are not a wine-drinking people and that the consumption of wine in this country must have a limit. Perhaps that is so, but, in my opinion, we are very far from being within sight of that limit. The reply I receive to so reasonable a claim is that a sufficient appreciation of wine is not to be found except among a very small section of the public; that the number of connoisseurs is negligible; that wine is a luxury and only for the few or, as *such* protagonists probably miscall them, *hoi polloi*. What ridiculous nonsense! You can make any-thing a luxury if you make it expensive enough: Mr Gladstone said that before I did. In days of scarcity people gave pound notes for bananas and oranges, and tea was a luxury until wise statesmanship made it plentiful and cheap and the daily (hourly?) stand-by of the cottage-dweller. You can pay sixty or seventy thousand pounds for a Titian or a Gainsborough, but pictures of one sort or another adorn practically every dwelling in the country. The connoisseur does not create an art nor make it a luxury, but he keeps the culture of it alive, and, though he himself indulges in the best his means permit and his taste allows, he encourages, by his example and precept, a wider interest in the particular branch of art which appeals to him. So is it with wine. We should encourage an abundant choice both for the delectation of the connoisseur and his cronies and for the health, enjoyment and enlightenment of the many, who may themselves one day be connoisseurs.

Another South American country that would like to send us wine is Argentina. The possibilities over there must be immense from the point of view both of soil and climate. The Argentine is a considerable importer of wine and one would have expected it to be a considerable exporter, but one hears very little, or has heard in the past very little, of its viticulture. True, I was a shareholder in an Argentine Railway Company at one time which paid no dividend but never failed, in its glowing annual report, to extol the quality of its ever-increasing production of wine. Alas! in those days I saw neither wine nor money. During the War, now happily closed, I was invited to an *almuerzo*, at a well-known London restaurant, to taste and discuss *algunos vinos argentinos*. There were several of us, in a room below ground, and the host and some of his guests were people of more than ordinary distinction. At many dinner parties, particularly in restaurants, it became fashionable before the War to serve champagne as an *apéritif*, and sparkling wine, called erroneously, and I could almost say unaccountably, champagne, was served on this occasion, but I am glad to report that all the other wines were served under their own names, including *Cabernet reservado* (which, in my opinion, was the best wine of the lot, being the most natural), *Pinot Superiora viejo* and *Riesling* 1934. On the whole I was sadly disappointed. Some of the wines were fair, it is true, but I am sure the Argentine can do better than that, both in red and white varieties; and, if I be asked what my chief criticism of them was, I am inclined to opine that they had been too carefully, but not too skilfully, treated. They had been obviously prevented from developing themselves naturally in order that they might be canalized towards *tipo* this or *tipo* that, which, in my opinion, was a pity. Let this magnificent generous country, to which the imaginative and the enterprising, and sometimes the too-enterprising, of all the nations of the world are drawn, employ some of these immigrants' brains, energy and knowledge to produce and send us wines fit for our tables and of *tipo argentino*. They might have a great future.

CHAPTER 13

Chevalerie

Anjou and Touraine. The Bold Baron de Luze. Chevalier de la Légion d'Honneur. The Retort Discourteous. A Highland Gathering at Oxford. Lord Tweedsmuir.

Having mentioned the white wines of Alsace, I would be doing less than justice to France were I to omit to say a word about those of Anjou and Touraine – which might be red as well as white – and it will be only a word. They were brought very much to the notice of the wine trade by my friend the late Alec Wood, who came and asked my advice as to the best and most promising methods of marketing them; and I have no doubt he consulted others of his friends also. He showed me several samples of still, light, white beverage wines of varying degrees of natural sweetness, and I came to the conclusion that they were good enough to stand on their own merits and told him so. He had been advised to 'baptize' them with such Bordeaux appellations as 'Vin de Graves' and 'Barsac d'Anjou' and so on, but, happily, I was able to dissuade him from such an errant course and during his lifetime the wines made good progress under the names of Anjou. I hope room will be found for some of them in our Government's post-war 'concessions' of wines from France.

I have never had the good fortune to visit the historic châteaux and vineyards of the Loire in spite of many pressing invitations from my old friend, and leader in the Anti-Prohibition League, Baron Raymond de Luze, of Saumur, with whom I have enjoyed many a glass of his excellent Ackerman-Laurence, which displays so many of the sparkling qualities of champagne – and of good champagne at that – without its supreme touch of aristocratic refinement. Raymond was deputed by the French Embassy in London, during its occupancy by that genial and affable ambassador M de Fleuriau, to decorate me with the Legion of Honour. The ceremony took place at a small dinner party, and what a gay one! Only eight or ten of us including Raymond and Madame la Baronne (an American lady), the Simons, my partner Nevile Reid and his wife and Hilda and myself. Towards the end of dinner, Raymond rose from his place and took up a position at one end of the room: he then summoned me to join him and we stood facing each other, at about six paces apart, like a couple of duellists. For a few minutes Raymond, speaking, I think in English, though I cannot remember, told me what a fine fellow I was, how I fought and bled for France, and how zealously I propagated, by precept and example, the virtues of her vinous riches. Suddenly he drew himself up and, in French, called me to 'attention'; then in the name of his great and beautiful country, he pinned the coveted decoration on my breast. Having done so to his satisfaction, he, formally and with sacerdotal dignity, kissed me on both cheeks and then shook hands with me cordially, as a good old friend and comrade, amid the plaudits of the rest of the party. I was, and am, a proud *Chevalier de la Légion d'Honneur*. Then we reseated ourselves at the table, and glasses were raised to France and Britain, to those present and to those absent, while I taught them all the words and tuneful lilt of a jolly students' drinking song we used to sing fifty years ago in Bordeaux:

> *Pendant qu'il filera*
> *Et son voisin s'apprête,*
> *A la pomponnette, à la pomponnette*
> *Il fi . . . . lera!*

the hiatus between '*fi*' and '*lera*' being long enough for the toasted student to empty his glass.

Raymond has told me, more than once, of one of his recollections which is worth repeating. When he was a young fellow he was sent over to a family in England to polish up his knowledge of the English language and of life in this country. With his connections, he had no difficulty in finding a temporary home and welcome in a typically English country mansion, where he met many young people, and where he had opportunities for tennis, riding, shooting, fishing and the usual amenities of the country gentleman's life. He told me he thoroughly enjoyed it all and that, when he had at last, and much to his regret, to say goodbye to his charming, hosts, he told them with emotion how happy he had been and how grateful he felt, adding, with true French gallantry, 'If I were not a Frenchman I would like to be an Englishman'. One can imagine his surprise, his hurt surprise, even if tinged with a shade of admiration, when one of the sons of the house exclaimed, 'If I were not an Englishman I would shoot myself'! It is clear that that little expression of discourtesy, so thoughtlessly uttered and, of course, so unintentional in its rudeness, has never been forgotten.

There is another white wine from that part of the world to which I was first introduced by Walter Berry. It is called Pouilly Blanc-Fumé and must not be confused with a white burgundy which is also called Pouilly. This Loire wine, when young and fresh, and served cold, is very attractive with its sensation of bubble, or liveliness, that the champagne people would call *crémant*, creaming. I doubt whether it is a wine likely to improve with age as it is rare to find, and I have myself never left it long enough to attain maturer years. The fact is it is too nice when young to be allowed, perhaps fortunately, to grow old. I once heard a story of an enthusiastic bridegroom who, on his wedding day, said his wife was so sweet he would like to eat her: the story goes that ever afterwards he wished he had. Pouilly Blanc-Fumé might be similarly disillusioning? It may be safer not to give it the chance.

Having interpolated Scotch and Irish Whisky into my comments on white drinks, although they have nothing in common with tendrils of the vine, I feel inclined to recall an occasion in Oxford on which a milk-white liqueur was featured. It occurred during my command of the Argyllshire Territorial Battalion of the Argyll and Sutherland Highlanders. I was sitting one evening in the library of the house we then occupied, near the old Crystal Palace, when in walked one of my junior officers, Jock MacDonald of Largie, accompanied by another splendid young Highlander, Neil Ramsay. They had just come all the way from Oxford to ask me if I would attend the 'Varsity Caledonian Society's Dinner the following evening, in place of the Secretary for Scotland, who was to have been their guest of honour but had just cried off. I had practically refused, when Lorne came in and said he would be attending the dinner himself and would drive me there and back. Further dalliance was impossible, and down we went. John Buchan, M.P. (later to become Lord Tweedsmuir), was the other official guest; we were piped into the big dining hall of one of Oxford's famous inns and found ourselves in a company of some fifty or sixty braw young Highlanders clad in the garb of old Gaul of many clans, some Jacobite in appearance, with velvet tunics or scarlet waistcoats, lace jabots and ruffles, and all sorts and descriptions of ancestral ornaments in the shape of belts and horns and dirks – a really glittering, animated and colourful sight. Am I showing myself top professional when I say that one of the things I remember is that the claret, so called, was abominable; thin, tart, acetous, undrinkable, as far as I was concerned, and a disgrace to any hotel keeper in those days? It was all we were given, and I had a 'dry' evening, since, when the time came for coffee and dessert, we were served with a white creamy liqueur, by name Atholl Brose, very suitable perhaps for a Highland gathering, particularly with Neil Ramsay in the chair, but uninviting to one who is not habitually a liqueur drinker. Lorne said it was very good and counteracted the acidity of the wine! But I abstained. The climax of the evening came with the toast of 'The Guests'. This was received with full Highland honours, every man standing alert on his chair, with one foot on the table, and, while cheers echoed in the ancient rafters, there was a tintinnabulous crackle of splintering glass all round the room as fifty or sixty wine-glasses, thrown over their shoulders by the diners, struck the walls behind them and were dashed to smithereens. Fortunately wine-glasses were not so difficult to replace then as they are today, but the splashed mess of Atholl Brose that brightly dyed the walls, wainscoting and floor must have entailed countless hours of labour for the few days that followed. From that moment all was pandemonium, and speeches were almost taboo and quite inaudible. When I was called upon by the chairman to respond to the toast, I was greeted with mingled boos and cheers and cries of 'Sit down, Sir', 'That's enough', 'Cut it short'. I need not say I did, after a few appeals to national pride and patriotism which also had a mixed reception, boisterously vociferous. I anticipated that Buchan, being one of themselves, would be differently treated, but he fared no better and was perhaps even more brief. It was not an occasion for polished oratory, and he knew the Oxonian buoyancy of spirit, and Highland at that, and I feel sure enjoyed it as much as I did. When Lorne and I had to make a move to get back to Norwood, our car was surrounded by our gay and noisy hosts, and we drove off amid a storm of cheering which increased to a rapturous hurricane of yells and hurrahs when two streamers of diaphanous paper, not generally displayed in public, unfolded themselves from rolls, which had been cleverly fixed on each side of the car, and floated after us into the evening air as we made our way triumphantly and with all possible speed, along 'The High'. I think some of those gallant, jolly boys must have had headaches next morning after the sour claret and rich liqueur; history does not relate; but many of them, I know, have given their lives for their country in the War. Buchan, I always maintain, wrote one of the most felicitous volumes of pure English literature of modern days, *Montrose*; and it is I, a Campbell, who say so. He is not only historically fair and impartial, but combines with historic sense language that lends colour, life and lucidity to a fine literary exposition of conflicting loyalties and ideals. A great Scot of whom those Scottish undergraduates at Oxford were rightly proud.

CHAPTER 14

Champagne is so Elevenish

Mrs Campbell and Oxford. Champagne as *Apéritif.* E V Lucas. Old
Champagne. A Case of Spontaneous Combustion. Inter-Wars Vintages.
Ice, Corks and Ullages. A Story of the '15. Sidetracked.

I suppose we all have pleasant recollections of Oxford: I have
many, as Lorne was at Merton, old George Saintsbury's college,
and my wife and I were frequent visitors. At a still earlier date, I
remember, I had to go to Oxford on business and took my wife
down to the Mitre with me. We were sitting at dinner when
H D G Leveson-Gower ('Shrimp') and Colin McIver, who was
in the now defunct firm of Bridges, Lloyd and Routh, came in
and found us enjoying a bottle of champagne. I at once made
quite unnecessary excuses by pleading that my wife was very tired
and that I had ordered it for her benefit. This, of course, led
to more champagne being opened because 'Mrs Campbell is so
tired', and from that day to this many of my cricketing friends
inquire, when they meet me, after Mrs Campbell's well-being,
whether she is tired and what vintage we are now patronizing.
I think the champagne famine of the War years will probably
have sealed the doom of this solicitude for the state of my wife's
health! There is no doubt about it, champagne is the finest of all
pick-me-ups, and the first glass of it you drink (no heeltaps) after

a period of strain or fatigue is as welcome and uplifting as the divine nectar. Perhaps Barry Neame and his coterie have been right to offer champagne as an *apéritif* instead of the obnoxious cocktail, though one cannot get away from the fact that it is also without a rival for detonating the sometimes obdurate catherine-wheel of conversation at the dinner table. There are many men I have known who before the War drank champagne every day of their lives, if they could get it: one very well-known member of the champagne trade even used to boast that he never went to bed without having had at least one bottle during the day. He was a great sportsman and lived to a ripe old age.

That writer, too, of beautiful English prose, E V Lucas, with whom I used to sit on the Committee of Surrey County Cricket Club at the Oval, was a persistent champagne drinker. He had a *penchant* for the widow Clicquot but condescended sometimes to enjoy other brands. What good work he did for *Punch* and other publications, and those short pen sketches of his that appeared from time to time in the former were veritable literary gems sparkling with wit. I congratulated him once on the perfect style and phrasing of one of them and was surprised when he told me he had taken tremendous trouble over it. 'We all talk bad English', he said, 'and generally write as we talk. I do the same, and so I rewrite and rewrite until I am satisfied with the bit of work in hand.' 'Genius', said Carlyle, 'is a capacity for taking trouble', and E V L certainly demonstrated it. His private letters were comic in appearance, as the first line went right across the page and each succeeding line was shorter than its predecessor until he wound up with his name or initials in the bottom right-hand, or left-hand, corner. Our president at the Oval in those days was 'Shrimp' Leveson-Gower, who is also an admirer and good judge of champagne and a spritely and most entertaining after-dinner speaker. I think his favourite brands are Dry Monopole and Bollinger but he is not so fastidious and exclusive as E V L was, and we have shared some of what might be called the 'lesser lights' together. He is a walking encyclopædia when it comes to cricket.

I suppose the majority of people imagine that they would like to have been the merchant to whom I alluded above and drink champagne every day of their lives. I think they might be disappointed. Champagne, I know, would pall upon me if I *had* to drink it every day. And yet, and yet! That one cold, full, fresh, fizzing glass of champagne at the psychological hour, and most people put that about eleven o'clock in the morning, or just before the evening dinner, could, I believe, be an almost irresistible daily treat. But as the normal accompaniment of my meals I personally would always choose a still wine – and preferably claret.

My experience is that no similar record of the champagne one drinks is kept as in the case of clarets and burgundies, and I am afraid, and always have been afraid, that champagne would lose a lot of its intellectual interest for most of us if the competition in it were confined only to shippers' brands and not to vintage years as well. Champagne becomes *passé*, in public estimation, while it is still comparatively young. At twenty years of age a *cru classé* of claret may be just reaching its prime and a robust vintage port be still in its boyhood, but champagne, at that age, is considered old and 'beery' or 'metallic', though, as a matter of fact, if it has been lying in a cool cellar or, better still, in the cold chalk caves of the Marne, it can still be young and fresh and vigorous.

I had the good fortune to drink in Bordeaux, in 1892, the Clicquot 1875, of high renown, and the Perrier-Jouët 1874, which, at that time, my father declared was the finest champagne in his experience. They had been sent there from Britain but were even then deemed to be long past their best and on the decline. We had some old champagne of about that period, perhaps '75, in one of the London homes of my earlier days, but we had also a man and his wife on the domestic staff, and all I knew about the champagne was that it was rapidly disappearing, because, according to my information, of a mysterious propensity to burst! Surely a clear case of spontaneous combustion if there ever was one! So I may say, with some certainty, that the 1874 Perrier-Jouet, a wine of grand quality, is the oldest champagne I have tasted, but in 1892 I was too ignorant really to appreciate it; and the same plea of ignorance saves me from having to criticize 1875. Leaving out intermediate years – though Moët shipped some remarkably fine cuvées in the 'eighties – I come to 1892 and 1893, which I sampled quite abundantly, and both of which had a most enviable reputation at the time. The 1893 was by nature so sweet and forward that it perhaps lacked backbone: it certainly came to maturity before the 1892 which was a very well-bred, beautifully flavoured wine developing and ageing with grace and deliberation. I much preferred it to the highly esteemed and expensive 1889s, even after the latter had overcome the unmistakable hardness and severity that characterized them in their early days. 1895 vintage should, by all the conventions of commerce, have done, but did not do, the champagne trade a power of harm, as the wines were constitutionally unsound and liable at any moment to go completely out of condition. We all know how some of them were reported to have been offered 'thick' or 'clear', on the analogy of soup, and, although Krug suffered from the prevailing malady less perhaps than some others, I know we were thankful when the wine had disappeared. My readers will remember how heavy and sooty a deposit the 1895 burgundies threw, and some climatic disturbance may possibly have affected both them and their more northern fellow victims in champagne. Most champagne houses shipped 1898 and 1900 but the two wines of that period that most appealed to me were the Clicquot 1899 and Pommery 1900. The latter was superb, of noble character and flavour, while the former possessed a nutty nucleus, of fruit and flavour, more coquettish perhaps, which has often led me to say that it was the most attractive champagne I have ever tasted; a perfect gem. Curiously enough, I found a similar nucleus of fruit and flavour – minus the coquetry! – in Krug 1926, and, when my friends ask me which was the finer wine, Krug 1926 or Krug 1928, I have to ask for a bottle (or preferably a magnum) of both to help me to make up my mind! One of my keenest competitors, Henry Rivière, agent for Louis Roederer, and the memory of whose friendship I cherish, came up to me in Mark Lane, soon after we had offered the Krug 1928 on the market, and said 'Ian you are the limit: I have gone about saying that your 1926 is the best champagne ever made and, damn it all, your 1928 is better'. He was no doubt right up to a point as all the 1928 champagnes were good and it is only a question of personal preference that excuses discrimination. When I encountered wine merchants at the time we were selling the 1928 and they questioned me as to how it compared with the 1926; 'Please do not ask me', I used to reply, 'I exhausted all my epithets on the 1926!' Yes, omitting the superlatives, Henry Rivière must have been right. I doubt if there was ever another vintage like 1928 of which it could be said so truthfully that all were good; but, obstinate fellow that I am, the '26 was worthy of admiration too, but not perhaps so universally. 1929, most opportunely proved itself a thoroughbred and better stayer than anticipated. Some of the brands compared favourably even with their own 1928.

At the battle of Alamein, the 7th Bn Argyll and Sutherland Highlanders, under the command of my son Lorne, pierced the enemy's front and captured a German Brigade Headquarters where they found many luxuries, including food and drink and ladies' silk stockings. They brought Lorne a bottle of Pol Roger 1926 which, he wrote me, tasted 'heavenly even out of a tin mug'! These Germans thought they had Cairo in their pocket and had prepared themselves to enjoy to the full the ripe fruits of victory.

There was a large assortment of vintages of champagne imported into this country between the two Wars, and 1911, 1913, 1914, 1915, 1917, 1919, 1920, 1921, 1923, 1926, 1928 and 1929 had all been shipped by one House or another: people paid their money and took their choice, capable of turning a deaf ear, it is to be hoped, to the cajoling recommendations of second-rate restaurant waiters, whose main source of knowledge used to be so often the scale of remuneration they might receive for pushing certain brands in preference to others. Happily the restaurant authorities and the champagne trade together determined to root out a foreign practice which was probably as fleeting as it was objectionable. I hope we shall hear no more of it. The 1919, 1920, and 1921 triad gave rise to no little controversy and some confusion in the public mind. All three were undoubtedly fine wines. 1921 may be described as of good breeding, but rather plain and stolid, with a shade of hardness that did not disappear with age. 1920, aristocratic and delicate in style, remained pleasing and refined even in declining years, and was probably the best of the three. 1919, more plebeian, but with many of the good qualities of the 1920, was at one time almost equally popular.

Fashion is fickle, and all champagne brands have had their moments of popularity and their days of indifference; curiously enough, too, certain parts of the country seem to be wedded to one brand and other parts of the country wedded to another, while neither of these brands may be particularly favoured in a third part of the country. I have pleasant recollections of many brands of many vintages. I have already mentioned a few and could add largely to their number if my memory were not getting a bit rusty. Pommery 1904 for instance, which combined a fullness of vinosity with the charm of delicate flavour, was, as well as the 1900, a great favourite of mine, and the early development of Roederer 1920, which I placed high in my tastings, could be best described as making it racy and carefree and very good to drink. I had a warm corner for a long time for Ruinart père and fils 1913, and, to come to more recent years, there were few of the 1926s I thought more highly of than Ayala; and to mention just one more, Pommery, with their 1929, which is very good, have made a bold bid to re-establish their old brand. But there is not one of what I look upon as the dozen or so of crowned heads of Champagne that did not produce royal wines in abundance during the inter-war years, and it would clearly be invidious, impertinent and absurd for one who is a champagne agent himself, to make any real attempt to compare the respective merits of his competitors' masterpieces. I omit all mention of the postwar shipments now *sub judice*. Once, when my doctor had forbidden me to take any 'alcoholic refreshment', a birthday, or some other anniversary, occurred and I had to tell him that I had disobeyed his orders and given myself a glass of champagne with the best results. He laughed heartily when I added that the champagne had 'reanimated my inside' and said he would try the experiment on others of his patients.

Some people, and particularly ladies, like champagne to be served very plentifully iced, which is a mistake if it is the flavour of the wine that is to be admired and not merely its fizziness: excess of icing has the same deleterious, deadening, effect on white wines that excess of chambré-ing has on red, and both extremes should be sternly avoided. Another common error amongst champagne drinkers is hastily to blame the shipper for an occasional 'corky' bottle; the shipper has selected the best corks he can, and if now and again a bad cork manages to pass the very severe scrutiny it is an unfortunate accident, 'just too bad', as the Americans say. I admit, of course, that a 'corky' bottle of champagne (or any other wine for the matter of that) is undrinkable. An 'ullaged' bottle, on the other hand, that is one from which a little wine has leaked out round the cork, which is also severely criticized, can be quite drinkable if the ullage is neither excessive nor of old standing: I have enjoyed many an ullaged bottle of champagne, but claret on ullage is detestable and how often one is given it in private houses! A bottle of any wine will become 'ullaged' if kept for a length of time standing on end, a position which will allow of, and even create, an air hiatus between cork and liquid. All wines therefore should be stored in the horizontal position.

Champagne, as I think is generally known, is made from the

juice of both red grapes and white grapes, judiciously and carefully blended so as to avoid too much colour and body on one
side or too little colour and lack of fruitiness on the other. The
big champagne houses draw their grapes from the same vineyards every year and thus develop a style and character of their
own which make them recognizable to the expert. When the
1915 vintage champagnes were being blended M Joseph Krug
was a prisoner of war in the hands of the Germans; in close con-
finement, as he had attempted more than once to escape – and
curiously enough, along with him was a gallant brother officer
of mine in the Argyll and Sutherland Highlanders, the late
Maclean of Ardgour. In M Krug's absence his wife, Madame
Krug, a brave lady, whose courageous and beneficent work in
the two great Wars has been more than once recognized by a
grateful France, did the blending. She evidently favoured the
red grape as she produced a much fuller bodied and deeper-
coloured champagne than was usually connected with the
name of 'Krug', but we sold the entire cuvée of 1915 in record
time. Even those who expressed surprise at the change of style,
when they heard the reason thereof, came chivalrously forward
and claimed their share. A year or two after the wine had been
shipped we had a call from Colonel Sarson, of Leicester, one
of the leading and best-known experts in the wine trade of his
day, and *not* a 'Krug' partisan. He came, however, to ask us
if we had any of the 1915 left because he wanted some more
of it: his allotment had been a very small one. 'But', said I,
much astonished at so unusual a request from such a quarter,
'it isn't a typical Krug'. 'That's the reason, I think, I like it so
much' was his quick and unanswerable reply. Sarson was a keen
Territorial as well as a shrewd man of business, highly respected

and popular in the best sense, and passed away not many years ago at a very advanced age. The 1915, owing to the richness of the blood of the red grape perhaps, was inclined to get heavy and taciturn as it became old, but we shall always be gratefully mindful of Madame Krug's loyalty and resource and her private *cuvée*'s instantaneous success.

I remember the first time I went to Reims; it was in the spring of 1893, and I was going there on my way back to England from Bordeaux. The porter at the Gare de l'Est, in Paris, did not inform me that I had to change, at I forget where, to go to Reims, and I was carried on to Hastières on the Belgian frontier, having already been frightened out of my wits by the invasion of my compartment by a gang of cardsharpers who endeavoured, almost with threats, to get me to play with them. I refused obstinately, however, and they eventually quitted the train to try their skilled hands no doubt on more easy prey. I felt an awful fool, all the same, when I found myself at Hastières and made inquiries about getting back to Reims. I framed a brief wire to Paul Krug, father of my good friend the present head of the House, in which I said that I had been *dévoyé* and was arriving at such-and-such an hour. It was only later that I discovered that the verb *dévoyer* is rarely used except with reference to an unfortunate girl who has 'gone astray'! Truly, a little knowledge is a dangerous thing, and my *petit faux pas* must have caused a good deal of amusement to the *famille Krug* when it reached them.

CHAPTER 15

Oporto: Wine, Women and Tobacco

Oporto. My Dress Clothes. Trade Etiquette. The Factory House. In re Wine-Glasses. Mishaps and Merrymaking. Crusted and Wood Ports. Ladies and Smoking. Dissertation on Smokes and Wine. A Stray Shot.

My first visit to Oporto, which took place in the autumn of 1897, produced even a more foolish huddle on my part. As I always have done, and still do, when travelling, I packed my own luggage before leaving home, but when I was in the train between London and Liverpool, from which latter port my steamer to Leixoẽo (Oporto) was sailing on the following afternoon, I suddenly realized that I had left my dress clothes out of my box: it was a horrible discovery. I dashed out of the train at Rugby and sent off a wire to my people requesting them urgently to send the absolutely indispensable articles of apparel to the steamer in the docks. My anxious inquiries, when I went aboard next afternoon, however, met with a blank response, and we sailed without my dress clothes. I was furious with myself and the evil genius that must have blinded my eyes to the clothes that were all laid out ready to be packed.

All the big bosses at that date of the port wine trade in London seemed to be going over to Oporto by the same opportunity, for the purpose, I have no doubt, of passing judgement on the 1896 vintage wines, already highly spoken of, and perhaps also to draw a bead on the newly made 1897, which promised well and had the added advantage of synchronizing with the Diamond Jubilee of Queen Victoria. I felt very shy in the company of such celebrities as Moncrieff Cockburn, Francis Croft, Cecil Page, Ramsay Dow and his partner Silva, Yeatman (the 'Professor'), Harry Newman ('Noggs') and the editor of *Ridley's Wine and Spirit Trade Circular*, Harry Sparham, who had a bigger reserve of funny stories than anyone else I have met in my life. There were others in the party whose names have escaped me, but it was a truly great and representative team, and I think I am right in saying that Cecil Page and Francis Croft swam ashore from the boat when we entered the harbour of Leixões. I inquired at Messrs Graham's offices next morning whether the parcel with my dress clothes had arrived overland and the soft answer in the negative did not turn away nor dispel my wrath. Charles Adam and James Yates were the directors of Graham out in Oporto at the time. Yates had lost his right arm in a bicycling accident some years previously but had become so deft with the other that one hardly noticed it except when shaking hands with him. He was also one of the cleverest and best informed port wine men of his day and only died quite recently, full of years and honour. He and Charles Adam, who seemed to me a dour Scot if ever there was one, had married sisters of the name of Atkinson, Yates's wife being the widow of Gilbert Elles who had also been with Graham. There were, I was told, nine Atkinson sisters, all, or nearly all, of whom married into the port wine trade, which may have accounted for some of the secrecy and exclusiveness that seemed to keep the business establishments at arm's length from each other in those days. Certainly nine sisters – and what a good-looking family they were! – might, with the best intentions in the world, unheedingly create a babel of tongues and gossip pregnant with untoward and mischievous consequences. I remember, as an example of that apartness, that on one occasion, when I was in Graham's Lodges in Vila Nova de Gaia, across the river from Oporto, I mentioned to Yates that I was going along to Cockburn's Lodges to see a wine-merchant friend of mine from England who had told me I should find him there. 'Oh, you can't do that,' interposed Yates, with an expression of horrified anguish depicted in every feature, 'it isn't done: we never enter each other's Lodges.' A message, however, was got through to Cockburn's and I was invited to come round. I received a charming welcome from Moncrieff Cockburn and John Teage and found my friend, the late Russell Harvey of Bristol, there, and we all had a crack and a *boa pinga* of wine in the very pleasant surroundings. I have every reason to believe that nowadays the Oporto Houses work much more together than they then did. I hope so. Unity is strength.

The visit of the London contingent of port wine magnates was made the occasion for much junketing and entertainment, and I received an invitation to a banquet at the 'Factory House', the handsome old building which was the club house, I understood, of the most exclusively British *élite* of the port wine community. Be that as it may, the style of architecture, furnishing and appointments would have compared favourably with those of any London club I knew. I had reluctantly to refuse the courteous invitation owing to the deplorable deficiency in my wardrobe. Then it was that the true clannish character of the dour Scot came to light, and Charles Adam undertook to

rig me out with a discarded dress suit of his own: and, in spite
of discrepancy of height and figure, he did so, and I went to
the feast somewhat resembling, I fancy, those delightful Eton
boys who dash about the streets of Windsor in clothes that
make them all look as if they had grown a lot faster than their
parents had anticipated. The banquets in the 'Factory House'
are very ceremonious affairs but very jolly. I believe the rule
is that the annual president adds a presidential contribution
in kind to the wine cellar, and the consequence is a superb
series of fine wines, French, German, Spanish and Portuguese,
to accompany very remarkably good cooking. A procedure that
was a novelty to me, and a very laudable one, was the retirement, immediately after the sweets, of all the company present
from the dining-room to an adjoining room, where a beautifully polished old table had been laid out with decanters of
port and an accompaniment, amongst other decorations and
adornments, of rare delicate wine-glasses. Around this table we
all sat and, in more senses than one, discussed the port. It was
a very memorable experience for me, and for a while I was able
to turn my mind off my dress clothes and attune it to more
agreeable and inspiring measures.

Wine-glasses play an important part in the appreciation
of wine, and I recall those royal words which I quoted earlier
in these reminiscences, 'men of taste who were able to enjoy
the wine the more for the beauty of the vessel in which it was
served'. Glasses should be thin and delicate where they touch
the lips. I even prefer them also to have thin and delicate stems:
true, it renders them easily breakable in the hands of a clumsy
pantry-hand, which, forsooth, would break anything, but it
constrains the man (or woman) who drinks out of them to

treat them with suitable care and respect, which again may have some beneficially refining influence on his own nature. I am not enamoured of the stemless wine-glasses that the stringencies of the War have brought into use in clubs, restaurants and private houses during the last year or two. My vintage port neither looks nor tastes so well in them, and I hope they will disappear from our tables as soon as circumstances allow of the regrowth of the more elegant and endearing stem. I have heard it said that war is a necessary evil providentially devised to prevent the over-population of the world, but it is, in my view, a brutalizing and unsettling remedy, a product distinctly of human or devilish conception and the arch-enemy of all artistic culture and pro-gress. The world now wants a clear century of peace to recover from the iconoclastic distemper contracted during the last fifty years. The reappearance of grace and elegance, at and on, our dinner-tables will be one of the first signs of regeneration. The atmosphere of comfort, beauty and refinement pervading the 'Factory House' in Oporto on that never-to-be-forgotten even-ing impressed me deeply and has recorded in my mind an ideal to maintain. The nearest approach to that apotheosis of dignity and tranquil enjoyment that I can remember was when I dined at the high table in Trinity College, Cambridge, with my old schoolfellow George E ('Tommy') Moore. I was surrounded by Intellectuality (with a capital I), dons, masters, wardens, who treated the port wine ritual with studied reverence, but relaxed solemnity, in keeping both with the antiquity and architectural grandeur of their surroundings and the doffing, for a few pre-cious, gladsome, hours, of the mortar-board and gown of a stern erudition. Yes, they did enjoy their vintage port, '70, I think, and so did I.

My dress clothes followed me to Oporto all right but failed to arrive till after I had started for Bordeaux on my way home; so they pursued me to Bordeaux and thence to London, where they turned up safe and sound about forty-eight hours after I did! The poet Wordsworth seems to have foreseen the episode and its happy termination when he sang:

> 'Though mean
> Our object and inglorious, yet the end
> Was not ignoble.'

I generally encountered some sort of mishap on my visits to Oporto. I went there once when there was a smallpox epidemic on, or so it was alleged, and was recommended to be re-vaccinated. I was, and the serum 'took' very badly, gave me a temporarily paralysed arm, and utterly ruined my enjoyment of a big ball – given in the ideal setting of the 'Factory House' by my friends Max Graham and his wife, wonderful host and hostess, in a fairyland of illumination and floral decoration, with good music, good floor, good dancing, good champagne and a gay and happy social throng. On another occasion I took my wife with me, and she developed mumps when we disembarked at Lisbon. I could not leave her at the Avenida Hotel so had to send her to the British Hospital, a drab establishment where the only literature to hand was a copy of the Common Prayer Book, wholesome, no doubt, but not a bright antidote to the pain and discomfort of mumps. Meanwhile I went to the Max Grahams' rose-garlanded home in Oporto to share with Max his daily quota of delicious old port, ageing in wood but plummy, vigorous and vintagy, as well as various other vinous delicacies. He and I went to the railway station a week later to meet my wife, now pronounced immune. For safety's sake she had swathed her head in a loose summery bandeau of chiffon, or tulle, or whatever it is called, and, as she came out off the platform, Max caught sight of her and exclaimed with horror, 'She's got them still!' We had a few days merrymaking in Oporto, and these little incidents, aggravating as they are at the time, only add to the joy of pleasant memories.

There is as much amusement and instruction to be culled from the guessing of port vintages and shippers as there is from the guessing of claret vintages and 'growths'; and my experience is that one makes equally ludicrous bloomers, particularly, as in the case of clarets, too, when one comes to deal with modern vintages. Nowadays we drink and enjoy these, perhaps rightly, when they are much younger than we were wont to in bygone years: circumstances have probably guided us a good deal in this direction: the lack of shipping during the years of war has forced the consuming of port wines already in our stocks, and many of these would be wines fairly newly bottled, such as crusted, or crusting, wines (and how good and palatable some of them are, or were) and vintage wines. 'Crusted' ports would cover all those of vintage character which are put into bottle when young and full enough to throw a 'crust', or more or less firm deposit, on the inside walls of the bottle. 'Vintage' wines themselves would come into this category, of course, but are singled out as the *crème de la crème* of certain selected super-excellent years. Some crusted ports I can remember were most delicious drinking after being kept in cask for four or five years and then 'under the cork' (ie, in bottle) for another five or six years. They ripened sooner by reason of this than did the early bottled 'vintage', and, having been allowed to develop rather longer in wood, they had already lost, before being put into bottle, something of their body and robustness. It seems to me a great pity that the taste for these economical, invigorating and attractive wines has apparently died a natural death; or have prohibitive custom duties, and the motor car, and the abominable hustle and bustle of modern-day existence had something to do with it?

In Oporto, owing to climatic conditions, they drink port straight from the wood, and of late years it has become more and more fashionable to do the same over here, if vintage port is not available or if ladies are present. Why this latter proviso I know not, because I find that ladies enjoy and savour appreciatively the 'vintage' wine though, owing to its being heavier, and perhaps a little more heating in consequence, they limit strictly the quantity they will take: and who shall blame this self-denial? Not I. More than half the pleasure of drinking good wine would be lost were the enjoyment of it not shared with others; nor is it any longer *de rigueur* for ladies to feign an ignorance of, or lack of interest in, wine.

And, *apropos* of the ladies, I am often asked my opinion about smoking and its repercussion on wine, and I may mention at once that I am a non-smoker. I was once rude and drastic enough, as host at a small dinner-party at Elm Grove, Ockham, to request the lady sitting on my right to stub out a cigarette she had hastily lighted just as I was starting the port wine decanter going on my left. I had, as a matter of fact, opened a special bottle of 1896 vintage port for her husband, just home from the Far East, who was sitting next to my wife at the other end of the table. This was evidence enough of my anxiety as to the effect of the tobacco on the wine. The lady took my rebuke, or remonstrance, or rudeness, whichever it should be called, in good part and drank and praised the wine, and I am sure it was sheer thoughtlessness, or force of habit, perhaps, that had led her to light up at that stage of the dinner. I think many smokers are similarly thoughtless and have no express desire or intention to be selfish when they swap cigarettes and light up during a meal. I am, as are others, not a smoker, but I am very tolerant of tobacco, which obviously gives pleasure to so many, and am ready always to accept the sociable compromise that the first glass of port should go round before cigarettes or cigars are produced. Unfortunately that 'gentleman's agreement' has gone by the board since the fair sex took to smoking. Wherever you go now, even in private houses, where in my young days smoking was taboo until host or hostess gave the invitation to smoke, the tobacco habit flourishes and Milady Nicotine reigns supreme.

The problem for hotels and restaurants is admittedly difficult. I have had a good deal of insight into fashionable restaurant life during the War, and there I find that Algernon and Evangeline toy with a cigarette, or two, with their cocktail, or two, before sitting down to dinner, and indulge in a cigarette again after the oysters or soup, with another to follow the main course, and yet another with the sweets and the coffee, whereafter Algernon probably calls for a cigar and the pageant of smoke is slightly varied. I see also, not infrequently, four or five people who are dining together round a table, with a decanter of claret – regardless of expense – in the middle and claret in their glasses, take out their ornamental cigarette boxes, exchange cigarettes and smoke voluptuously while they quaff their wine! I am afraid the members of neither of those two parties have given one thought to neighbours who possibly might be trying to appraise the flavour of a bottle of claret or burgundy or vintage port. They would be shocked and hurt if it were suggested that they were selfishly spoiling other people's physical and cultural enjoyment. We wine-people have to grin and bear it and are not encouraged, in an anticipated atmosphere of smoke, to satisfy our somewhat fastidious taste in wine. Smoking need not accompany food as drinking should and does, nor would our wine-drinking impair the enjoyment, by other diners or ourselves, of a smoke, after dinner or in the lounge or veranda; but the fumes from a single cigarette will permeate a whole restaurant and tend to vitiate, in some degree, the flavour of every glass of wine therein, not only at the time of ignition but for hours afterwards. The remedy lies with the restaurateur who may one day have to choose between smokers and wine-drinkers; some, I am glad to say, have already done so and forbid smoking in the dining-room. In clubs and private houses also it is good to find that the artistry and delicacy of wine are still generally, though not universally, recognized and respected. There, at least, observance of the 'gentleman's agreement' should and could be upheld. A pipe is still considered 'bad form' even in a restaurant, though I must say my sympathies are often with the home-coming warrior who carries it about with him as his *fidus Achates* and the one friend to which he can turn when looking for solace and contentment. Still, the smell of a foul pipe, however well-beloved, can hardly be tolerated as a companion to food and drink. To be quite fair in this matter of smoking and wine tasting and drinking, my experience is that a habitual smoker can be pretty well as reliable a taster of wine, certainly as consistent, as a non-smoker. The late

Mr R C Ivison, of sherry fame, in whose Bodega in Jerez-de-la-Frontera I enjoyed the advantage of having my first lessons in tasting, was admittedly one of the finest and most meticulous sherry tasters of his day, and yet he had a cigarette in his mouth all day long from the moment he rose at six o'clock in the morning till he blew his candle out at about eleven o'clock at night. He affected cigarette papers and loose tobacco and, like so many Spaniards, kept himself occupied during many hours of idle conversation, in and out of business, by rolling *cigarillas* and smoking them. I nearly shot him once by accident when he took me out to his shooting box, with a party of friends, to shoot rabbits at four o'clock on a summer morning. My old hammer gun went off when I was unloading and must have just shaved old Ricardo's head, as he gave a jump and emitted an ejaculation! In two seconds, however, he calmly replaced the cigarette he had removed from his lips and, with the unexpectedly quiet admonition *'cuidado, niño mio'* ('Careful, my boy'), broke into a peal of laughter. I think I got a bigger shock than he did. Others of my friends smoke a good deal while they are tasting, or just before, and their verdicts do not seem to be in any way jeopardized by it. They do not, of course, smoke while they are drinking wine or, at any rate, not until after everybody has had his first glass of port, and, generally, not even then; with the brandy, however, out come the smokes, and even I will admit that I think the fumes of a fine cigar blend harmoniously with the bouquet of fine brandy.

CHAPTER 16

Vintages and Bottlenecks

Harmony in Wine. Port the Englishman's Wine. Vintage Port. The Manly '96. A Centenary Luncheon. Eclipse of '97. Third-Year Bottling. A Gresham Club Luncheon. '31 Quinta Noval. 1934 and 1935 Ports. Vintage Bottling in Oporto. Bottleneck.

The allusion to harmony at the end of the last chapter brings me back to vintage port, the essential property of which, as of sherry, champagne and all blended wines, must be harmony. Like the Champagne folk, the port wine shippers get their young grapes either from their own vineyards or from vineyards equally well planted, positioned and tended: they will take, to utilize in their blends if suitable, the crop of the same vineyards year after year so that they, like the champagne shippers, have gradually established a style and individuality of their own which enables a clever connoisseur to declare the name of the shipper of a wine in spite of the natural diversity of character that distinguishes the product of different vintages. Even so, the verdict, and I speak with a knowledge of personal guilt, may be rather a matter of guessing, wine being, as I have said before, a living organism and variable according to how and where it has been kept, bottled and binned, and is served. I find the average wine-drinker in England far more likely to be able to give a correct vintage to port than to claret, which proves I think that port is still rightly called 'the Englishman's wine', though some of its best-known shippers bear Scottish sounding names, to wit, Cockburn, Dow, Graham, Mackenzie, Sandeman, and others. Scotland may not be able to boast the acknowledged name for bottling of vintage port acquired by so many of the provincial towns of England; but, on the other hand, Scotland, owing no doubt to her historic alliances with France, gained an enviable and well-deserved reputation for importing the finer claret. Lord Neaves it was who said – and shame upon him for the heresy:

> 'Mutton old and claret good were Caledonia's forte
> Before the Southron taxed her drink and poisoned her
> with port.'

We all know the alarming effect of 'the English Statesman's' *dictum* on the 'Caledonian'. The SPIRIT of the latter has, however, been reincarnated in a generous arid appeasing guise that has quite conquered the Sassenach!

I like my vintage port best when it has become old, but I find the port lovers of the rising generation like it much younger; I have no doubt they are right – we old fogies keep all our wines too long sometimes – and their view in any case is more in conformity with the economic post-war circumstances. The young wine merchant will tell me that 1927 vintage port, for instance, is at its best today and should be drunk now. In my opinion 1927 can be drunk and enjoyed today but will be much better, silkier and more choice to the palate, in another five, eight or ten years' time. My experience is that a good, well-balanced, vintage port – such as undoubtedly 1927 is – may become 'drinkable' when comparatively young but will remain drinkable, develop charm and improve in taste and character, for many years afterwards. May I take as an example, Dow 1912, a comparatively light wine but one of my favourites, which I could drink with enjoyment very soon after the close of the First World War and can drink with still genuine enjoyment today. Vintage port of very fine quality seems to me to have a staying power, a *joie de vivre*, which enables it to carry on and endure long after one might have expected it to vanish into thin air: Cockburn 1853, remarkably sweet and self-possessed even at sixty years of age, was completely forgotten long before that time by its own parents, the shippers: Martinez 1875 too was another 'light' vintage port which carried on with courage and aplomb – and a delicate charm – to an advanced age. I drank it at No 24 Mark Lane with pleasure and satisfaction till André Simon changed his address. I have no personal knowledge, of course, of the early days of vintages '53 and '75 but believe that the latter, certainly, was never looked upon as a 'stout fellow'. I do, however, very well remember the 1900, which Dow did not ship because they had just shipped an 1899 and we, Graham, did not ship because we preferred the rather less attenuated 1901. Our ethics and our wine were good, but the unilateral policy can only be a limited success. 1900s were pretty and elegant but very, very light and, at quite a young age, were placed on the obituary list. They were probably aided in their vanishing trick by the First World War demand, but, not long before the Second World War began, I had Cockburn's 1900 with Ernest Cockburn and Taylor's 1900 with Basil Dent and found them both full of flavour and delicious to drink. They had 'carried on'. A 'vintage' about the turn of the century was called for as four years had elapsed since 1896, and Providence and the port shippers, working hand in hand, seemed to have mutually agreed that there should be a supereminent vintage every fourth year, as for example 1896, 1900, 1904, 1908, 1912, when, unfortunately, war intervened and, as in the ease of champagne, irregularity and independent enterprise followed. When 1896s were first shown, in 1898, many old-fashioned wine merchants described them as wine and water! 'Nothing like the manly vintages of old times.'

'The "good old times" – all times when old are
good – Are gone.'

I doubt if we have since had so majestic and manly a vintage as 1896. The wines must have been forced into consumption too soon, for my taste and that of others, as large quantities were shipped and, when we emerged from the First World War, with tongues hanging out and thirsting for port, there seemed very little of any of them left. I do not remember coming across a bad 1896, and the baker's dozen (approximately) of 'vintage' ship-pers that I am accustomed to put in the front rank all shipped a front-rank wine. I liked them all and had a special penchant, as I think I mention elsewhere, for Cockburn and Taylor, both of which I considered superlatively fine and well able to hold their own with the giants of old: these two keen rivals both stood out prominently also in 1904, their wines lasting much longer than the majority of those of that rather disappointing vintage. Ferreira 1896 was another champion which might well be classified as superlatively good. It was served as recently as this year at the centenary luncheon of the agents, Cock Russell & Co, at the Connaught Rooms: I must say it drank splendidly and seems to be still full of vitality and fruit. Cock Russell's menu card on that occasion devoted one of its pages to an enlightening and very interesting comparative list of duty-paid prices of wines in 1845 and 1945. The list was headed by the caption, 'Comparisons are Obvious'. Here it is:

	1845	1945			
Sherry	40s	186s	per dozen bottles		
Port	45s	174s	„	„	„
Marsala	32s	180s	„	„	„
Claret	30s	150s	„	„	„
Burgundy	34s	150s	„	„	„
Champagne	90s	420s	„	„	„
Brandy	84s	444s	„	„	„

(*17 up in* 1845)

The 1945 prices being those of the wines and brandy imported under Government authority (!) while those of 1845 were no doubt taken from Cock Russell's own records of a hundred years ago. Times change and values with them, but the list shows what excessive duties and governmental domination will do.

I remember that, when lunching with my friends Harvey, of Bristol, in the upper chamber in Denmark Street, between the wars, Eddie Harvey said, 'I am including in the wines today two that were never shipped to this country'. The paradox became intelligible when we came first to the champagne which was Pommery 1911. This excellent specimen of a fine vintage had been offered to the trade by André Simon and his partners just prior to the outbreak of the First World War, but was withdrawn again by the Reims Principals when hostilities were in full swing, not, however, before a few lucky customers had been able to get over a part of their reserves. The second wine to which Eddie Harvey alluded came as a greater surprise and was announced as Cockburn 1897! It appeared that, before they had made up their minds not to launch 1897 as a Vintage, Cockburn followed a not infrequent practice in the old days of sending their friends John Harvey & Son a sample pipe out of their new vintage 'lot'. The wine was delicious, quite in the Cockburn tradition, and it is a pity that the abundance of the highly, and worthily, esteemed 1896 prevented the 1897 from being shipped and its attractive qualities meeting with the universal appreciation that was its due: I was lucky to be in the minority. Hastings Perkin, that shrewd independent judge and critic of all wines, always maintains that 1897 was really the finer vintage of the two, and Graham the best of the '97s, though I blush with confused modesty in repeating (in full agreement) this well-balanced verdict. The Sandeman 1897 was also a beautiful wine, and is still most pleasurable to drink, as I know to my own advantage. The vintage, however, was not generally shipped. Sandeman seem to favour off-vintages and were alone, I think, in shipping a 1911 which I found very much to my liking; and if, as some assert, it is passing sweet that does not seem to me to be a shortcoming. Was it not Coleridge who sang, for the benefit of so many of us:

> ''Tis sweet to him who all the week
> Through city-crowds must push his way'?

Port indeed, should err, if it err at all, on the sweet side, but I am well aware that there exists an opposite school of thought in the ranks of port wine shippers. To me a dry, really dry, port is almost a contradiction in terms. But *jam satis*! I am not here to argue: port must be opulent and generous.

The 1917 is another of those 'light vintages', that is occasionally met with, and seems to be plodding quietly and unostentatiously on although it has been proclaimed dead and buried years ago. Owing to shipping and other difficulties most of the 1917 arrived in this country right at the end of the year 1919, too late indeed for any quantity of it to have been bottled before the turn of the year, and so a large proportion will have been bottled in the early part of 1920. This is called 'third-year bottling' and is supposed to reduce slightly the market value of vintage wine which normally is assessed on a 'second-year bottling', that is, before the third winter has passed over it while it is still in the wood. Some important wine merchant bottlers, however, have almost invariably bottled their vintage ports in the third year, and I would mention Messrs Corney & Barrow as one of them, with very successful and satisfactory results, and I fancy that it would be to the advantage of the port wine trade were the taste for third-year bottling to be encouraged in the rising generation. The wine, it is possible, would lose something of its majestic volume, but nothing of its flavour, and would gain in silkiness and a somewhat earlier maturity. That pre-eminent port wine stalwart, the late Ernest Cockburn, expressed a similar view in a book of notes upon Port and Oporto which he had compiled shortly before his death and which, I hope, may some day be published for the benefit of the public. I think it would rank as a classic.

I had the Taylor 1917 quite lately and found it full of life and charm, but the vintage was only shipped by a few Houses: it will never be classed among the *élite*. Nor, I fancy, will 1920, 1922 and 1924, though they all produced good, even fine, wines. All are still very drinkable and on the light side, which is not a disadvantage if you get the right character and flavour and sufficient sugar. With my, I fear, failing palate I find it no easy matter always to distinguish between these three years and frequently take a toss. I make no excuses: it is better than the fellow who proposed to the wrong sister of twins – and was accepted!

Both Fonseca and Croft of 1922 struck me as being very attractive and, today, I would as soon drink the latter as any other port I know except, perhaps, a good specimen of vintage 1912, which in my judgement has not yet gone very far over the hill, say, a Cockburn or a Taylor or (may I whisper it?) a Graham; and I would include my Dow although it is no doubt deliciously descending the downward slope. A beautiful magnum of Croft 1922 was served at a small luncheon party at the Gresham Club given in honour of my son Lorne, on his return from the wars, by George Fraser, Edgar Walmisley and one or two other well-known members. 'Uncle Charles' Stevens and I were included as guests: I suppose that, as brother of one VC – Admiral Gordon Campbell – and father of another VC, I must occupy a rather unique position, and even the modesty I so often assume would hardly be justified in hindering me from showing and expressing my pride. The magnum, too, seemed conscious of the occasion and, after seeing that outstandingly attractive little St. Emilionnais, the 1934 Canon-La Gaffelière, comfortably and appreciatively disposed of, came to the front of the stage and took the 'House' by storm. Croft port, represented in England by Yool Bowes, delightful and devoted lover of the art of port, is rarely luscious, but is sufficiently sweet and very elegant, with body and flavour beautifully balanced, and the '22 is typical and induces one to pinch the lobe of one's ear in the manner of the Portuguese people when showing approval.

The 1927 is the vintage of today, and its advent, sponsored admirably as it was by all leading shippers, brought back memories of those fascinating rivals 1908 and 1912, each in its way so distinguished, so alluring and so invitingly responsive. I am not sure that 1927 is quite as good as either, but it is in the same succession, and it is difficult to find a bad one among the lot. War conditions, and the consequent dearth of older wines, have brought the vintage early into consumption, too early in my opinion, but then, as I have already mentioned, I am a *vox clamantis in deserto*, most of my junior colleagues in the wine trade appearing to consider that it is already showing all the signs of senescence and should speedily be served, enjoyed and relegated to the pages of history.

One can hardly count 1931 as a 'Vintage', but it will be memorable for at least one wine, da Silva's Quinta Noval, which, like the 1921 Château Cheval Blanc in Bordeaux, stands out a giant among its contemporaries of the year; and it is a real giant, a son of Anak. I tasted it recently under curious circumstances, wherein a cellarman took a bottle out of a wrong bin and decanted the 1931 Noval, and sent it up to table as Sandeman 1890! Of course there was an immediate outcry of incredulous protests, but, instead of demanding the cellarman's head on a charger, we called for the cork, which was fully and correctly branded, and the honour of both Sandeman and da Silva was satisfied. The '31, though still in the chrysalis stage of 'blackstrap', is on the move; its colour tint veers from blue to brown, the first sign of adolescence, and one day it will be a thing of beauty and a joy for as long as it is allowed to last: there would be no compliment in saying 'for ever'. I believe the proprietors of the vineyard of Noval still boast the possession of pre-phylloxera vines: I hail them *o terque quaterque beati*! Bottling in the third or even fourth year of their remarkable 1931 would have been not only justifiable but, perhaps, even advisable, the wine is still so big.

There was an unwonted and unfortunate controversy over the respective merits of the 1934 and 1935 vintages, and eventually some firms shipped '34 and some '35, whilst one or two shipped both. Dow, Fonseca, Martinez and Warre were prominent in the 'thirty-four *bloc,* while Cockburn, Croft, Graham and Taylor were in the van of the 'thirty-five, and Sandeman and Tuke Holdsworth, I think, went boldly for the 'double'. Both vintages are decidedly above the average quality, but neither, it may be surmised, outstandingly better than the other, and the rivalry between them may be as long lived as that between the popular 1899 and 1900 clarets. Quite apart from, and in addition to, excessive Customs duties, already mentioned and censured, restrictions on shipment of port, imposed by our too timid Government 'in the national interest' during the war, have aroused misgivings about the future of vintage port, but several of the Houses in Oporto, quite alive to the danger, have been bottling their vintages on the spot and, although the outcome will not be altogether the same as if the wine had been bottled over here, I know, from my experiences of earlier vintages bottled and properly harboured in Oporto, that the wines will display the quality and many of the best characteristics connected over the years with vintage port and will nobly, pleasingly and competently, hold the field until normal conditions once again return. The Englishman's heritage of vintage port is far too precious to be endangered by folly, prejudice or neglect. It will be perceived at once that I am a Caledonian of the sterner stuff and still enjoy my port and the company of the good English friends who share it with me. Ernest Cockburn, whose too early death I so sincerely lament, was another Caledonian, 'stern and wild', who, until that fatal germ got the better of him, relished to the full both his claret and his port. His body, being mortal, was in the end overcome, but his spirit never. He recovered from bouts of intense agony with a joke on his lips and a kind thought for his friends. After losing his leg he wrote me on, a postcard: 'They cut off my right leg a few days ago! I don't mind that so much, but would you believe it – they did it WHEN I WASN'T LOOKING! All goes well, but it is pretty painful.' He was a born chief, a laughter lover, a good friend and a veritable pillar of the port wine trade.

There has grown up in these days of hurry and 'getting on with things' an increasing use of the word bottleneck; shipping has been a bottleneck during the war, Pakistan a bottleneck in India, the exit from Twickenham football ground was always a bottleneck, the threat of famine is a postwar bottleneck to world prosperity and the lack of babies the bottleneck to the survival of Britannia. In fact bottleneck has become a household word applicable to any let or hindrance, and it must, surely, derive from that funny little waist in the neck of a port wine bottle. I have made diligent inquiries – almost like a cabinet minister – but have not yet been able to find out how and when that kink was first introduced. The reason of it was no doubt to make doubly sure that no air should be able to reach and oxidize, or even impair, the precious liquid within the bottle, but it is a terrible nuisance and responsible more than anything else, I think, for bad decanting of vintage wine, particularly if it is old and the cork inclined to crumble: it is responsible, too, for the necessity to use muslin, more or less clean, which, in my opinion, always detracts from a wine's liveliness, and other expedients to prevent bits of cork and broken crust gate-crashing into the decanter and spoiling its contents. It is not everybody who has the means or the time for using those elegant long tongs, which have to be heated red hot before they can perform their duty, that of nipping off the upper half of the neck of the bottle, which a skilled operator will see that they do very efficiently though at the cost of a perfectly serviceable, and today exceedingly valuable, bottle. It is almost like setting a thief to catch a thief: you waste a bottle to circumvent a waist! Whatever the need for the kink may have been in bygone days, I feel sure that the introduction of the long cork has made it more of a nuisance than a necessity and that it could and should be omitted by makers of port wine bottles in the future. I willingly accompany my suggestion with an unqualified prospective apology to politicians, publicists and other persons likely to be affected by this threatened bottleneck to their flow of language and stream of similes.

CHAPTER 17

Sherry at Home

Jerez de la Frontera. The British Colony. In Ivison's Bodega. Something about Sherry. Ostracism. Return to Favour. Sherry's many Attributes. Sweet Scented Memories. R William Byass. Carl Williams. Strange New World.

The first occasion on which I remember drinking vintage port, apart from any I may have 'inhaled' when engaged in sending out the samples of Graham's 1887 already recorded, was in 1889 at a dinner party in Jerez de la Frontera, given by Don Pedro Mackenzie and his wife, two characteristically hospitable Scottish friends. Their son, Kenneth, then a wee boy whom I used to go to see in bed when I dined with his parents, is now himself the popular and respected Head of Mackenzie & Co of Jerez – and Oporto. Hence the vintage port, which I thought dangerously fascinating: in fact I remember being a little frightened of accepting a second glass, but it was a case of nothing venture, nothing win – and I won. I have no note of what the vintage was. The British Colony, as I knew it in Jerez in 1889, consisted of a small, very united, group of about seven families who seemed to vie with each other in making the stranger in their midst feel at home. I like to recall their names to my grateful memory: they were the families Buck, Davies, Mackenzie, Marks, Neumegen,

Warter and Williams, with singletons like Graham Gandell and Jimmie Gordon, student-visitors like Gilbert Forrester of Belfast and myself, and a chaplain for their own pretty little church at the end of a fragrant border of violets in the grounds of El Palacio, the home of the Bucks. Two chaplains succeeded each other during my stay in Jerez, and I was best man to one of them soon after my return to England, and the other, Basil Winter, was best man to me several years later. I went daily to the *bodega,* or overground cellar establishment – called *lodge* in Oporto – of Ricardo Ivison who was exceedingly hospitable and claimed, not unnaturally, to be of Scottish descent: he had a remarkably beautiful Spanish wife and a big family.

In the gable-roofed *bodega* with its rows and rows of butts I learned how to taste, select, classify and blend sherries. I found it most interesting and did not take long to grasp the differences between a *fino* and an *oloroso,* a *manzanilla* and an *amontillado,* and all that. I drank sherry daily in my diggings in the *Torneria,* right opposite the ever-open door of the family Williams' home, and in everybody's house I visited, and am sure I owe much of any knowledge I may have acquired about wine to the sound training and thorough grounding I received in Jerez. Ivison, of kindly heart but tempestuous spirit, had erected a brandy still on the premises of his *bodega* which was run by a Scotsman, called Stewart, who, by the way, could also be unrestrainedly outspoken in moments of excitement! And nearby there was, of course, a water tank which was about twelve or fifteen feet long, eight feet wide and about six feet deep when full, and therein I learned to swim. Herbert Buck and Forrester came occasionally and joined me in diving for pennies or bits of metal, this strenuous physical exertion being followed by a draught from the *'fino' solera*. Ivison's own boys were like seals in the water and most accomplished swimmers.

Sherry needs no acclaiming from the housetops today, with its popularity so well assured, in spite of flattering and clever imitators, many and menacing, but it spent nearly forty years in the wilderness of fashionable neglect and disfavour, from the eighteen-eighties to the nineteen-twenties. What brought it back to its present state of grace was the steady optimistic provision of consistently good quality and a bright little advertisement which informed the world that 'Sherry is a good wine at all times'. So it is. It can be drunk alone at almost any hour of the day, or as an *apéritif* before meals, or during a meal, or, in its sweeter blends, as a dessert wine after a meal; to accentuate its general utility one may add that sherry is refreshing as a thirst-quencher when drawn, by means of a *'valencia'* – a yard-long thin wispy handled sort of ladle made for the purpose – from the cool depths of the butt; and even more delectable, perhaps, when decanted from a bottle in which it has been maturing and softening peacefully for a score or two of years. I can enjoy and, when I can get either of them, do enjoy, Harvey's rich succulent 'Bristol Cream', with its so palatable after-dinnerish flavour, and Gonzalez Byass's pale, light, trim, impeccably dry 'Tío Pepe', an ideal accompaniment to that introductory chat before dinner which so many people spoil, at least in my opinion, by gulping down a succession of iced-hot drinks – oxymoronal drinks – collectively called cocktails. For the domestic decanter it would be difficult to find a more suitable sherry than a medium dry *amontillado* such as is shipped to this country by practically all the leading Jerez Houses. The word *amontillado* indicates of the kindred and stock of Montilla, a locality which gives its name to a particularly dry, austere, dominating wine too strait-laced, so to speak, to be desirable company alone, but an excellent mixer in modulated measures: it imparts the elegance, refinement, flavour and nuttiness which should characterize a fine *amontillado*. As I pen this honoured Spanish name again I catch a vision of the humorist who composes *The Times* crossword puzzles and would give as a clue 'a little mountain in trouble but with, as it were, anti-proverbial developments'. I feel sure the members of the BBC brains-trust would not fail to discover the correct solution.

The seven English ladies in Jerez (and Mrs Mackenzie would, I hope, forgive me, a fellow Scot, for embracing her in this national company) divided up the week with their 'at home' days, and I have pleasant recollections of many hard sets of tennis won and lost. It all seems very far away today, as do the avenues of orange trees that bordered some of the streets along which I walked to my different destinations. The orange trees at one period of the year bore their golden fruit, their shiny dark leaves and their sweetly scented white blossom all together, a perfumed memory that can never die. No member of the profession of wine in the last three generations can speak of sherry without allusion to the outstanding personality of William Byass. At over eighty years of age, Byass is the 'Father' and 'Grandfather' of the wine trade, an inspiring and delightfully unassuming friend and leader, worthy of the universal confidence reposed in him and the genuine affection in which he is held. It must be getting on for seventy years since he played in the Eton cricket eleven, and a curious coincidence is that Carl Williams, his second in command in the Sherry Shippers' Association, played for Harrow, but that was some years later. Carl is a mere boy still, and keen master of gun and rod, particularly the latter, so much so indeed that today I would feel inclined to call him the Kingfisher of the wine trade. He used to come home to Jerez from school when I was quartered out there and, at eighteen, considered myself a full-grown man.

I was hoping to go to Jerez again before 'twilight and evening bell', but six years' warfare have created an almost impassable bottleneck. There seems a great gulf fixed between pre-war and the present days: morally, intellectually, socially, politically and artistically we seem to have merged into a new existence and, so far, a less happy one; but we should not be afraid of the future; even the small fry amongst us, by giving of our best, without stint, prejudice or boastfulness, can aid in the task of modelling the edifice of this strange new world on the eternal principles of good will, industry, individual responsibility, service to the community and the encouragement of the Arts. Wine is an ambassador of good will; it is one of Nature's own contributions to the industry of Man and a faithful, valuable and willing servant of the public. Wine is itself an Art and can, and will, I believe, assist the return of a tired and sorry world to an era of sanity and tranquillity.

CHAPTER 18

War Years and Worn-Out Tendrils

Wine Trade and the War Years. Simon's Publications. Categorizing Wine Drinkers. An Anglo-French Story. Memoranda for the Wine Buyer. The Tendrils go into Winter Quarters.

The wayward tendrils would be failing in their mission were they to allow me to close without some reference, even if a rather cursory and egotistical one, to the six years of war, through the vicissitudes and hardships of which the much-harassed wine trade managed successfully to struggle and survive to the great advantage of a weary and nerve-wracked nation. The unexpected capitulation of France in 1940, and the occupation by Germany of the French Atlantic ports, bolted and barred the door to exports of wine from France and made hazardous those from Spain and Portugal, not to mention the far-off Dominions of Australia and South Africa. Ours was a tragic dilemma, especially when the Coalition Government placed a practical embargo even on the feasible imports of wine to this country. It was during the period of this ban that, in default of younger available individuals, I found myself assigned the position of chairman of the Wine and Spirit Association, proud, indeed, but very diffident about my ability to deal with the difficult and entirely novel situation, particularly as the Association itself required immediate and somewhat drastic overhauling. After having denied for many generations that there was any food value in wine, His Majesty's Government proceeded, with characteristic political logic, to place us under the Ministry of Food, but, in the same breath, declared that wine was an unessential luxury and could claim no priority for shipping space in war transport. During many weary and exasperating months we petitioned, protested, argued or negotiated at the Ministry, hovering between alternating hopes and frustrations while we saw vital existing stocks gradually but steadily disappearing. It was not until Lord Woolton himself, probably the wisest and most efficient food administrator since the days when Joseph the Israelite held sway in the councils of Pharaoh, King of Egypt, consented to receive me and hear at first hand, without official embroidery or abridgement, of our precarious plight, that tentative steps were timorously taken to save the situation. A small, very small, token importation of port, sherry, Australian 'Sweet' and South African 'Sweet' was authorized, subject to agreement on a scale of division of profit, a controlled price to the public and a guarantee of 'equitable distribution', with any 'Black Market' solemnly barred. Intricate and provoking as it was to operate, there is no doubt, in my mind, that Lord Woolton's insistence on 'equitable distribution' kept the small trader alive.

I will not dwell upon the nightmare of finding oneself between the devil and the deep sea, collaboration with the Government and acceptance of unpalatable measures of control on the one side and, on the other, the outraged feelings of an old and honourable trade and profession that rejoiced in its independence and flourished on individualism.

When Lord Woolton seemed to be becoming a little more aware of the full tide of public demand for wine, and a little more sympathetic towards our representations and requirements, he was transferred by Prime Minister Churchill to another office, and Colonel Llewellin, a country gentleman with whom, also, it was a pleasure to work, became Minister of Food. The change, however, in spite of the Colonel's obvious good will and determination to bring in more wine, now including French wine, did not put an end to irritating delays; rather did the introduction of high finance, and somewhat acrimonious inter-governmental *pourparlers* with European countries, cause further confusion and postponements; so that once again there began to ring in my ears the old Latin tag we learned to repeat at school, *dulce et decorum est pro patria mori.* But the wine trade did not go under, no, not even when an ungrateful people gave Churchill his marching orders and put a Socialist Government in charge of the destinies of the Empire, with Sir Ben Smith as arbiter of Britain's food and drink supplies. By the time the dust of the electoral battle had cleared away, and the joint spadework of Llewellin and ourselves was beginning to bear fruit, my successor-elect, Michael Gordon Clark, was, very happily, released from the Royal Air Force and took over the chairmanship of the Association for which his ability, training, go-aheadedness and innate sense of humour eminently qualify him.

My relief was immense. 'Men of age', wrote that wise old philosopher, Francis Bacon – still so good to read and so perennially sound – 'object too much, consult too long, adventure too little, repent too soon, and seldom drive business home to a full period; but content themselves with a mediocrity of success.' I think his Lordship puts the Colonel in a nutshell. May his epitaph add weight to the sincerity of my tribute of gratitude to members of the wine and spirit trade who accorded me such patient, loyal and generous support during my tenure of office.

'I shall remember while the light lives yet
And in the night time I shall not forget.'

One of my more pleasant recreations during some part of these strenuous days has been the jotting down of these vinous reminiscences, often without any notes or data upon which to base them: this has necessitated a good deal of, I hope justified, reliance on a memory which was gratifyingly retentive in the past but may perhaps by now be somewhat clouded over with the inevitable mist and variegated haziness of age. I apologize at once for the liability to err which I share in general with my fellow-creatures. I hope, however, that, in spite of human and personal failings, and an all-too-obvious lack of literary skill, I may have been able to impart some interesting and useful information, and perhaps given some entertainment, to those of my readers who wish to become students of wine. I was asked by one of these, who had read some of the earlier sheets of my manuscript, to add at the end of 'the book' a chapter epitomizing and cataloguing the hints I had given on selecting, buying, tasting and serving wine, but I am conscious that mine are only personal views: I would sooner leave the privileges of instruction to those who, with greater technical knowledge, are far better qualified to give it. The viticultural and vinous publications of M André Simon, our best-known œnophilist, written in better and more expressive English than most of us can command, form in themselves a practically complete encyclopædia of wine. I have introduced my readers to what I have ventured to call 'The Four Essays in Wine', which form already a conventional ritual with all lovers of wine though perhaps not with all wine-drinkers, and, although, in the manner of Wolsey, I may have blethered boastfully about *ego et opus meum* there is, as I have frequently protested, no idea of this being in any way a textbook. There exists, in my opinion, a difference, be it noted, between those who, very properly and naturally, like a glass of wine as something nice and pleasant to drink – we can and should all be in that category – and those who love wine, not only on account of its physical charms but as an art and treasured object worthy of more serious study than is usually given to it; who love to probe the depths and inner recesses of a wine in order to discover all its virtues and all its failings, to make allowances and excuses for all its shortcomings and, then, to praise or condemn it with the full joy and zeal of conviction. The difference between the two classes of drinkers may often be little more than one of degree, or even of the nuance of words, but it is there, and I take the opportunity it offers of repeating, by way of an illustration of nuances, a story so old that I cannot remember its origin, but which I still tell and which still seems to amuse my listeners. It is of an Englishman and a Frenchman dining together in a restaurant and getting into an argument about their respective languages. The Frenchman claimed that his was the older and more beautiful tongue, and the Englishman that his was the more practical and richer in expression. 'How, richer?' exclaimed the Frenchman, a little warmly. 'French is the richest language in the world; rich in idiom, rich in music, rich in metaphor' – 'But poor in words,' interrupted his companion. 'How, poor in words?' pleaded the Frenchman. 'I will give you an example,' said the Englishman quietly. 'You have the word *aimer,* to love, and you are obliged to "love" everything equally, *aimer, aimer, aimer;* whereas we have the word "like" which enables us to differentiate. For instance, here we are in this restaurant and I say to you, "I *like* my dinner, but I *love* my wife".'

'*Mais oui! Mais oui!*' cried the Frenchman, with a gesture of triumph, '*moi aussi, j'aime ma femme, mais … j'adore mon diner.*' I have no doubt that to my funny French accent is due much of the success of the little anecdote.

As regards giving an opinion on the selection of wines to buy, the choice multiplies and varies so surely from year to year that no hard and fast conditions can be laid down. I think it is wise always to bear in mind that second-rate wines of a good vintage year are generally safer, pleasanter and better value than the 'big noises' of an indifferent year, and that a good vintage year in one country of production is not necessarily a good vintage year in all the others. Current estimation of wine is apt to become all too soon out of date. Wines come and go, they live and die like human beings; early promise often disappoints, and early doubts, happily, often prove erroneous and unfounded. I was reading a book called *La Vigne* written by a Frenchman and published in 1878. He describes 1869 vintage clarets as *médiocres* while we now know they were very much the reverse, and 1875 as plentiful but of questionable quality. His embarrassing choice of riches at his pet restaurant was between 1864 Ch Lafite and 1870 Ch Latour – in 1878! *Parbleu!* He proves the folly of too impetuous prophecy, and my advice to the would-be buyer, or embryo cellar-builder is frequently to consult a good old-fashioned wine merchant, whose knowledge and experience have dictated his own purchases and who will gladly talk about wine and the everlastingly intriguing problem of the younger vintages. He can support his opinions by practical demonstration (in times of Peace, I mean) and produce samples for your tasting, but, believe me, the best teacher will be the bottle you open in your own house; you will soon register your own likes and dislikes and the difference between *aimer* and *adorer*. George Saintsbury displayed constructive wisdom when he introduced to his cellar very small quantities of many and varied wines which, in leisure hours, he studied, enjoyed and discussed with his fortunate friends. You can do the same.

And so we draw to a close.

'The Bird of Time has but a little way
To flutter – and the Bird is on the Wing.'

The wayward tendrils droop dangerously in their upward climb and throw out silly curly fingers to clutch but empty air, for nothing more solid comes to their eager grasp. It is not their fault, poor willing emissaries, but that of the parent plant from which they sprang and which has ceased to provide the vital nourishment and lapsed into a state of comfortable comatose exhaustion. Cæsar had a word for it in those days of gentlemanly warfare, *hiemare,* 'to go into winter quarters'. The old vine stock that survives the cold hardships of winter will break into leaf again with the coming of spring, and the pathfinding tendrils will recapture joyfully their magnetic charm and guide the timid branchlets, with their sweet-smelling blossom, to wheresoever a bunch of grapes may safely nestle. There, in the providence of God, sheltered by fragrant leafage from too bounteous sunshine or blistering hailstones, the grapes will placidly grow and, sugar-full, ripen until they are plucked by the hand of the master and carried away to be converted into the wine that maketh glad the heart of man.

The tendrils have completed their task: let us accompany them into winter quarters. Till the spring? Who knows? In any event there will always be wine.

Index

WINE WRITING AT ITS FINEST

ON BORDEAUX
Tales of the Unexpected from the World's Greatest Wine Region
Susan Keevil
Why these wines are the most talked-about.

CHATEAU MUSAR
The Story of a Wine Icon
Serge Hochar and the most famous wine to come out of Lebanon.

IN VINO VERITAS
A Collection of Fine Wine Writing, Past and Present
Susan Keevil
The quintessential browsing book for those who love wine.

STEVEN SPURRIER
A Life in Wine
The incidents, adventures, ideas and discoveries that formed a remarkable wine journey.

THE STORY OF WINE
From Noah to Now
Hugh Johnson
The new edition of Hugh Johnson's captivating journey through wine history.

SHERRY
Maligned, Misunderstood, Magnificent!
Ben Howkins
This sun-drenched wine returns to our lives with a flourish.

WINE TASTING
Commemorative Edition
Michael Broadbent
The definitive guide that began it all.

10 GREAT WINE FAMILIES
A Tour Through Europe
Fiona Morrison MW
An up-close and personal insight into Europe's most celebrated winemaking families.

VIKING IN THE VINEYARD
Stories from a Revolutionary Winemaker
Peter Vinding-Diers
Six decades of wine adventure: Peter's pioneering exploits from Stellenbosch to Sicily.

CLASSIC EDITIONS
IN THE VINE COUNTRY
Edith Somerville & Martin Ross
Anglo-Irish cousins and writing companions set out on a harvest-time journey through the vineyards of Bordeaux.

www.academieduvinlibrary.com